ISRAEL--
Key to Prophecy

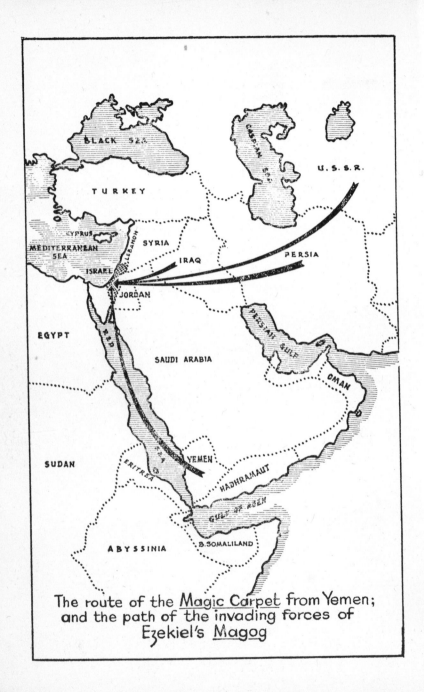

The route of the <u>Magic Carpet</u> from Yemen; and the path of the invading forces of Ezekiel's <u>Magog</u>

ISRAEL--
Key to Prophecy

The Story of Israel from the
Regathering to the Millennium,
As Told by the Prophets

by
WILLIAM L. HULL,
Author of *The Fall and Rise of Israel*

". . . the heathen shall know that I
the Lord do sanctify Israel, when my
sanctuary shall be in the midst of
them for evermore."

—Ezekiel 37:28

ZONDERVAN PUBLISHING HOUSE
Grand Rapids, Michigan

Second Printing — 1958

By the same author:
THE FALL AND RISE OF ISRAEL
*The Story of the Jewish People
during the Time of Their Dispersal and Regathering*

Printed in the United States of America

To my children,
WILLIAM,
BARBARA-ANN,
ELIZABETH,
RUTH,
this book is
affectionately
dedicated.

PREFACE

Recent changes and developments in the line-up and spheres of influence of nations have brought a situation so closely approaching the one indicated in the Bible for the last days that the conviction comes increasingly that we are at the end of this dispensation.

The establishment of the State of Israel, the reaction of Arab and Communist states and changes and discoveries in the world have revealed interpretations of prophecy hitherto largely hidden or veiled to Bible students.

This book interprets prophecy in the light of recent events, many of which clearly indicate the approaching advent of the Lord. It is intended as an antidote to the misunderstandings caused by the increased credence given to postmillennial and amillennial teaching in these last days. To leave out the nation of Israel as the future recipient of God's blessing not only makes the Word of God of none effect but also completely distorts it so that prophecy has no meaning. Only by understanding the part Israel plays in God's plan for this world can we understand the Bible. *Israel is the Key to Prophecy.*

The reader will note the sudden change from past to future events. Part One consists almost entirely of fulfilled prophecy; prophecy fulfilled, in fact, in the last eight years. Hence the use of the past tense. In the second part, after explaining the set-up of the nations, and from there to the end of the book, future prophecy is discussed as though it has been or is being fulfilled as we consider it.

There is no intention on the author's part to be dogmatic about the minor details of the fulfillment of prophecy, which he has depicted. Neither is it his intention to prophesy concerning the fulfillment of these details. This book is offered as a reasonable and possible pictorial revelation of future events connected with the land and the people of Israel of which their prophets spoke.

The use of the name, Joshua Ben-Elohainu (Jesus the Son of our God), for the name of the High Priest in the restored Temple under the Antichrist, has no particular prophetic significance or connection. Such a name could be possible in the Hebrew language presently used in Israel.

The main purpose of this book is to stir in the reader the realization of the imminence of the Lord's advent and the need to be spiritually ready for that event. At the same time the author desires to show the important part that Israel as a nation will play in the final salvation of the world and why they are a "chosen people."

When the Son of man cometh, shall he find faith on the earth?

WILLIAM LOVELL HULL

Jerusalem, Israel
December, 1955

CONTENTS

PART ONE

GATHERING HOME

PART TWO

EAST VERSUS WEST—WILL RUSSIA ATTACK AMERICA?

PART THREE

ISRAEL AND THE ANTICHRIST

Part Four

Israel and the Messiah

ILLUSTRATIONS

PART I

GATHERING HOME

> . . . I will bring thy seed from the east,
> and gather thee from the west; I will say
> to the north, Give up; and to the south,
> Keep not back.
>
> Isaiah 43:5, 6

Chapter One

THE DIASPORA AND THE PROMISE

For more than eighteen hundred years Israel languished in exile. To all exiles thoughts of home can bring periods of nostalgic anguish, however beautiful, peaceful or desirable one's exilic home might be. And Israel's lands of bondage had scarcely ever been desirable.

Exiled Jews had died in bondage far from home, leaving memories of Jerusalem and *The Land* to be passed on eternally from father to son. Thus the oft repeated phrase, "Next year in Jerusalem," became not only a hope and a pious wish, but a Holy Grail to be obtained eventually only through perfect faith and faithfulness.

Yet, idyllic as the thoughts of Israel might be, and however desirable a return to that land might appear, there were other and more pressing reasons why Jewish communities longed to find the way to cease their exile. God, through His prophets, had warned Israel that *He* would scatter the nation. "Like as corn is sifted in a sieve,"[1] God had warned that He would scatter and sift Israel among all nations. From the time of the destruction of the temple, in 70 A.D., this sifting had gone on, until one could scarcely find a land without its Jewish community.

It could hardly be said that in any land Jews had found continuous freedom and a peaceful life. At times, such as during the Golden Age in Spain, when for over two centuries Jews enjoyed such complete liberty and opportunity that Jewish natural ability and artistic temperament rose to the surface as at few times in past history — at such times Jews lived normal lives. Yet this period of peace was immediately followed by the terrible suffering of the Inquisition, and finally deportation.

In fact, Jewish suffering probably exceeded that of any other nation in all human history, and that for over a more or less continuous period of nearly nineteen hundred years of exile. In the ghettos of Europe, in the squalor of oriental communities, in the *Russian Pale* with its frequent pogroms, during the time of Hitler's hideous purge, even down to this day Jews have cried unto God from the depths of their suffering in the Diaspora. It has been but little more than fifty years that Jews have found in America the opportunity to live truly peaceful and unfettered lives.

In the midst of their oppression and suffering through the centuries one fact served to sustain life and to give hope even in the depths of despair. God repeatedly promised in His word that the day would come that He would regather Israel in their own land.[2] Hence the Jews constantly affirmed their hope of the realization of that promise — "Next year in Jerusalem!"

Chapter Two

FROM THE EAST

By the close of the nineteenth century events had already begun to conspire toward bringing the Jews back into their own land. The Balfour Declaration, issued by England during the First World War, and the subsequent release of the Holy Land by the forces of General Allenby, advanced the return to Zion. It was not, however, until the setting up of the Jewish state in 1948, that the doors were flung wide open to Jews from all parts of the world.

Then the promise of God contained in Isaiah 43 began to come to pass. "I will bring thy seed from the east,"[1] was the pledge God had made. East of the Land of Israel Jewish communities had existed for millenniums. There was no limit to the penetration of Jewish traders through the centuries, so that Babylon, which contained the first Jewish community in the east,[2] was but the forerunner of many other settlements. The Babylon community was mostly the result of capture and deportation, but the communities of India, Afghanistan, Malaya, China and other eastern lands were chiefly the result of Jewish search for trade and subsequent settlement in those lands.

In the East Jews suffered much less than the Jews of Europe. Yet they too longed for the day when their nation would be gathered home again. With the establishment of the State of Israel, Jews began to stream back to their land from each eastern country. From far off China thousands were flown in or came by ship. Most of these Jews had come to China in the last decade or two, refuges from Naziism or Communism. For them the open door of Israel was providential. Indian Jews came, many of them looking more Indian than Jewish. Some came from the ancient Cochin Jewish settlement, with their strange dress and oriental form of worship.

The largest ingathering of all was that from the Arab land of Iraq. This is the land of ancient Babylon. When the Babylonian captivity of Judah came to an end, many Jews returned to Israel under Zerubbabel.[3] Later, others followed under Ezra and Nehemiah. Nevertheless, a substantial number chose to remain in Babylon. Centuries later those in Babylon were joined by Palestinian Jews forced to flee from their homes. Especially was this so at the time of the destruction of Jerusalem in 70 A.D. and

Bar Kochba's defeat in 135 A.D. The size of this community fluctuated through the centuries. In 1948, at the time of Arab-Jewish war, there were about 135,000 Jews in Baghdad and adjacent parts of Iraq.

As Zionism developed, resulting in an increasing immigration of Jews into Palestine and a parallel increasing of Arab opposition, the lot of Jews in Arab countries became difficult. Iraq was no exception. The writer well remembers visiting Jews in Baghdad before the Second World War. They were afraid, even at that time, of showing any interest in one who came from Jerusalem. The Jewish position in Baghdad became increasingly difficult during the Arab-Jewish war and, with the signing of an armistice between Israel and most of the Arab nations, the Jews of Iraq petitioned to be allowed to go to Israel. The answer of the Government of Iraq was to pass a law freezing all assets possessed by the Jews of Iraq. Among Baghdadian Jews were those of great wealth. It is estimated that the total property seized by the Iraqi Arabs from the Jews was worth five hundred million dollars. The frozen assets were declared to be the property of the Iraqi government and permission was then granted to Jews to leave the country upon their renouncing their Iraqi citizenship, and promising never to return.

A giant airlift was organized to carry the Jews from Baghdad to Lydda airport in Israel. At first, however, Baghdad would not let any planes clear directly for Lydda, or land in Baghdad if they came directly from Lydda. They insisted on the planes going to Cyprus and there transferring their passengers to other planes for the flight to Lydda. This involved considerable hardship and a much greater flying distance. Eventually, however, Iraq permitted the planes to fly directly to and from Baghdad and Lydda.

Before the Baghdadian Jews began their airflight the Iraqi completed their plundering of them. Not satisfied with having seized the Jews' property, homes, businesses, bank accounts, stocks and bonds and everything they could get their hands on, the Iraqi searched each individual at the airport. Pens, watches, jewelry, currency, overcoats, all things of value, were taken from the Jews and each Iraqi Jew arrived at Lydda entirely destitute. For months such immigrants were arriving from Baghdad at the rate of almost one thousand a day and had to be provided with all the necessities of life. Yet they were back "home" after such a long time, and the President, Dr. Weizmann, could say, "Now we see the end of the Babylonian captivity!" Rich or poor, they were gathered back and God's word had once more proved itself to be infallible.

Chapter Three

From the West

The promise of God to regather the Jews embraced the four corners of the earth—north, south, east and west.[1] It is significant that a different word was used for the gathering from each point of the compass. Thus, for the East He said *avi*, "I will bring." No resistance or hindrance is suggested in this gathering, and none was encountered. Even in Iraq, once the Jews had made up their minds to leave, the door was opened for them to go without any actual physical hindrance.

For the West God used the Hebrew word *acabtsecha*, "I will collect" (assemble, gather). The West contained thirty times as many Jews as contained in the East. Yet the ingathering from the West has not been in proportion. Thus we see that "to bring" indicates a sweeping ingathering; while "to collect," indicates a selective ingathering. This is the way it has happened. From the West, a handful here, a few from there.

In the West, the largest center of Jewish life is in the

United States. In fact, this country, with over five million Jews, has the largest Jewish community in the world, far exceeding the number of Jews in the State of Israel. One would expect that Jewish emigration from the United States would have been in large figures as soon as Israel's gates were open, but this was not the case. In the four and a half year period from the founding of the new State, in which period the population of Israel more than doubled, the United States contributed but 0.6 per cent of the total immigrants, as compared with 23 per cent from eastern lands. God literally *brought* them in from the East, but He has been *selecting* them from the West, just as the prophet said.

There are two reasons for the small number of American Jews who have responded to the call of Zionism. First is the fact that Jews in America are too comfortable to be disturbed. They prefer the "fleshpots" and easy life of America to a pioneering life in Israel. For them Zionism is a theoretical proposition, a "backdoor" charity for their poor relations. The second and by far the most important reason, is that God still has a use for them in the United States.

It was not by chance that for three-quarters of a century America's doors had been open to Jews fleeing from the pogroms of Russia and Poland and from persecution in other European lands. It was not good fortune, nor even excessive labor and industry which has enabled American Jews to accumulate great wealth. Though by no means having the power and wealth attributed to them by anti-semites, yet the total wealth of the Jewish people in America is considerable. It is considerable because God has given it to them. Consider the words of Moses to Israel, ". . . thou shalt remember the Lord thy God: for it is he that giveth thee power to get wealth, that he may establish his covenant . . ."[2] At no time in Israel's history could the words of Moses be truer than during the last half century. The amazing ability of the Jews in America

12

1. The sign in front of the Israeli soldier indicates this advanced position as 10 kilometers from Ismailia on the Suez Canal.
2. Israeli soldiers in Sinai examine captured Russian arms used by the Egyptians.
3. Mr. Ben Zvi, President of Israel, Mrs. Zvi and Israel soldiers at Sherm el Sheikh on the Southern tip of the Sinai Peninsula. These Egyptian guns blocked Israel shipping in the Gulf of Akaba.

4. *Cochin Jews from India arriving in Israel by air.*

. *A Jew of the Habanim Tribe from Hadhramaut near Yemen.*

6. *A Hadhramaut Jewish silversmith receiving his first lesson in Israel in vegetable growing, from a Roumanian Jew.*

to establish themselves in business and to succeed where others fail, may be more a question of God's blessing than natural ability.

When the State of Israel came into existence on May 15th, 1948, the total Jewish population was 655,000. Within four and a half years a additional 707,650 Jews had come into the country. Most of these had come in almost as destitute a condition as the refugees from Arab Iraq. They had to be provided, in many cases, with shoes, clothing, beds, bedding, homes, furniture, kitchen equipment and many other things. Employment had to be created for the men, schools provided for the children and hospitals for the sick. Teachers, doctors, nurses, instructors, all had to be supplied in increasing numbers. Soon immigrants were arriving at the rate of one thousand a day. One thousand destitute, starving human beings; among them were many small children, tired, sick, crying. All had to be fed, housed and finally integrated into the new State.

If the people of Israel had had to depend on their own resources it would have been impossible to provide for such numbers of immigrants. Sufficient that the people of Israel shared their food, clothing, homes and other essentials with the immigrants. The resulting shortage of food necessitated a ration rate at the lowest of any civilized country. Space came at a high premium. Even if there had been a surplus of food and clothing it would still have required immense funds to build homes, schools, factories, etc. In other words, it was required of God that in fulfilling His promise to regather He should also provide in Israel for those He had gathered.[3]

It is estimated that it has cost three thousand dollars to integrate each immigrant into the economy of Israel. Thus, seven hundred thousand immigrants will cost over two billion dollars before they are fully established as self-supporting and productive citizens of Israel. From only one source in the world could such a sum come at this time — from the pockets of American Jews. God gave them power to get wealth, so that their wealth would be available to establish and execute His covenant with Israel — the establishing of His people in their own land.

Thus God is only *gathering* or *collecting* certain chosen ones from the West at this time. With the discovery of oil and the prospect of balancing the imports with exports by 1960, the day may soon come when Israel can be independent of United Jewish Appeals (UJA) and other fund raising efforts abroad. Provided, of course, that another large wave of refugee immigrants does not come in the meantime to further delay the time when Israel will be self-supporting. When this time comes God may do more than *gather* western Jews. There may be an incentive then which will not only make them willing but strongly desirous to come home to Israel. At that time they may be happy that the door of their native land is open to them.

Chapter Four

THE NORTH WILL GIVE UP

The situation in the North was different from that in the rest of the world. Hitler's activities had covered much of that area and by 1945 there were six million less Jews for God to bring to Israel from the north. With the gates of Israel open the surviving remnants from the concentration camps were soon on their way to Israel. Poland, Bulgaria, Yugoslavia, Hungary, Czechoslovakia and, in part, Roumania, permitted Jews to leave for Israel. But Russia, where now dwelt the second largest body of Jews in the world — Russia would not part with her Jews. Anticipating this, the language of the prophet concerning the north was, "I will say to the north, Give up." *Taini* was the Hebrew word. It is in the imperative — *Give me,* a command. The command has not yet been given and over two million Jews remain either willingly or unwillingly in Russia. Indications are that when God compels Russia to open her doors for the Jews to leave, the majority of them will take advantage of the opportunity.

Soon, it may be, the population of Israel will again be more than doubled. This time it will be by an influx of Russian Jews. It is doubtful that they will be permitted to bring much with them. It will probably be Baghdad-Arab treatment repeated. In any case, more homes, schools, factories, fields will be needed in Israel. More American Jewish dollars will be necessary to provide these. God still needs a great fund of wealth in American Jewish pockets.

Chapter Five

FROM THE SOUTH — MAGIC CARPET

In the English translation of God's promise through the prophet Isaiah we read, "I will say ... to the south, Keep not back."[1] The Hebrew word is pronounced literally, *altichlahi* "do not restrain" (hold back). This is also in the imperative, a command. It indicates a condition in the South unfavorable to the Jews, but shows that God will lift any restraining hand that might be laid on them.

Of greater interest in this direction, however, is the fact that God mentions here an individual country by name. In the case of the other points of the compass He specifies — east, west, north, in that order. But when He comes to the South He does not mention that direction. The English translation has obscured this interesting fact by substituting the word "south." The Hebrew, however, uses the word *Teman,* which is the Hebrew name of the country called in English Yemen. This is a southern country, it is not the Hebrew word for south. Thus God has literally said here, "I will say to Yemen, Keep not back."

Yemen is a land in the southwest part of the Arabian Peninsula. It is bounded on the north by Saudi Arabia, on the east by the Hadhramaut and on the south by the British protectorate of Aden. The Red Sea is the western boundary of Yemen.

In order to fully appreciate how realistic was the fulfillment of this prophecy one must know something of the background of the Jews in Yemen. They were a remarkable community. There is no definite historical record of when the Jews went to Yemen. Traditions place the time from forty-two years before the destruction of the First Temple to as late as the first or second century A.D. One story is that a large Jewish army had gone on an expedition into Arabia before the destruction of Solomon's Temple. They captured Sanaa, the captial city of Yemen, and remained in that land. Later, when Ezra returned to Jerusalem to build the Second Temple he sent word for them to come back to the Land of Israel and to help in the work. Tradition says that the Yemenite Jews refused to return at that time for they knew that the Second Temple would share the fate of the First. They are reported to have said that the time for the Messiah to come had not yet arrived.

In the fifth century A.D. the king accepted Judaism as the religion of the land, which at that particular time was called Himyar. The last king to reign in independent Himyar was a Jew. After this the Ethiopians ruled the land, then the Persians, before the coming of Islam, early in the eighth century, to conquer the land. Under Mohammedan rule the Jews became second-class citizens and life became difficult for them.

Some of the restrictions upon Jews were that a Jew could not ride a beast of burden, for that would raise him higher than a walking Moslem; he could not build a house higher than a Moslem, nor raise his voice before him. He must pay a special head tax and live in a ghetto. The Jew was regarded as unclean by Moslems. He had to rise before a Moslem, greet him first and always walk on his left hand. Special dress was required for a Jew so that he could not conceal his identity. He had no legal protection. A Jewish child left an orphan was immediately taken from the Jews and raised up a Moslem. Up to the time of the final departure of the Jews from Yemen it was forbidden for a Jew to leave the country. Any who where able to steal out were unable to take property or belongings with them.

As a result of their poverty, mostly caused by the intolerable restrictions under which they lived, Yemenite Jews became small of stature, thin and emaciated. At the time of their final departure the weight of the average adult was from seventy-five to eighty pounds. Yet, in spite of their hardships, they remained a kindly, likable and patient people. They were always religious and clung closely to their Torah in spite of all restrictions and difficulties.

Their study of the Law was somewhat hindered by a shortage of scrolls. There were no printing presses and all their Bibles were hand written on parchment. To offset, in a measure, the shortage of Torahs the Yemenite Jews sat or stood around the scroll and learned to read it from what ever angle they saw it. Thus they learned to read not only from right to left as Hebrew is written, but also with the scroll upside down (from left to right), or from the right side (upwards on each line), or from the left side (downwards, towards the reader).

The writer had heard several times of this strange reading ability but had never seen it demonstrated, until one day an old Yemenite Jew, still in his oriental clothes, came into the mission with his son, a young man about twenty. They wanted to see a New Testament in Hebrew. Without noticing, I had handed the book to the young man upside down. He opened the book from the left side, which would be the back of a Hebrew book held in an upright position. Then I noticed that it was upside down. Instead of turning the book the right way he seemed to pretend to read it. I thought to myself that probably he could not read Hebrew and that he was just trying to deceive me. I asked the young man how long he and his father had been in Israel. He replied, six years. This was the time of the great airlift from Yemen and I realized that here was one of those I had read about. It actually may have been easier, or at least as familiar to him to read the book upside down as the right way. He told me he could read also from either side.

The Yemenites, realizing that they were living in exile from their homeland, earnestly longed for the day to come when Messiah would deliver them. Their longing for redemption made them credulous to the claims of various false messiahs, who had risen up from time to time during past centuries. More than once they thought that the time had come for their deliverance, only to be disappointed when the claims of the imposter were proved false.

The country was taken from the Turks at the end of the First World War and it became an independent nation under the Iman Yahia. Influenced by Palestine Arabs, he made the restrictions on the Jews increasingly harsh and strengthened the restrictions against their leaving the country. Their lot was little better than that of slaves. Yet it was not the hardships of their life which inspired them to uproot themselves and leave. Something suddenly stirred within them and from over eight hundred different points in Yemen, cities, towns and villages, Jews began to move toward Aden.

God said in His word that He would say to Yemen, "Keep not back." When the time came for God to speak, the King of Yemen actually obeyed God. With the whole Arab world against the Jews and, even after the armistice agreements, still only waiting their chance to annihilate Israel, an Arab king permitted the Jews to freely leave his kingdom and to go to Israel. Except for the various head taxes paid to the sultans of the different territories through which they passed, and the hardships of the flight through a barren land, little actual physical hindrances occurred. However, many died on the way or in the camp from the hardships of the journey.

Some of those who had managed to escape from Yemen in years gone by had made their way to Aden. Due to Arab restrictions the ports of Yemen had been closed to them and Aden offered the only hope of getting to the Holy Land. Then, under the restrictive immigration policy of the British White Paper on Palestine of 1939, exit from this port, too, was barred. As a result these refugee Jews from Yemen gradually grew to a sizable colony in Aden of four thousand or more. When the mass move from Yemen began in 1949, a refugee camp had to be established near the city of Aden and at times as many as thirteen thousand were huddled together in this barren, windblown, desert camp.

Almost a Biblical account of how a spontaneous move started among the Yemenite Jews is contained in a letter written by one of the refugees. The account is contained in the excellent booklet entitled, *The Exodus from Yemen*. We give it in full, for no words of ours could convey so well the atmosphere of this Messianic event. This is how the writer discribed the exodus:

We lived in Exile, waiting for the Redemption to come, and did not know that it would come. There was one who went to the capital, and he returned with the tidings: "There is a State in Israel." And we knew not whether his tidings were true, Several days passed without a voice and without a sign. And during last year rumours increased, and men kept coming from afar and saying, "There is a king in Israel." Afterwards they said, "There is an army in Israel, an army of heroes." And finally they came and said, "The pangs of the Messiah — there is war in Israel." And we remained in Exile, and knew not whether the tidings were true, hoping for the Redemption, but the spirit was impatient... We rejected the Exile, and it was as though the spirit of the Lord rose within us: "Come let us go up to the Land of Israel." Now and again we asked: "Is there news of the Redemption?" And they said to us: "Wait, for the vision is yet for the appointed time."

Twice this year came the tidings that the Redemption was near, and many sold all their possessions, and set out on the way. And only the third time, everybody left with the permission of the King. The tidings came by letter, but in the letter was written, saying: "Urge not on the end." But we were already prepared, and many with their possessions rolled up in sacks, waiting for the sign, and there was none... And upon a day came a letter from the *Shaliah,* saying:

"Arise brothers, and arouse yourselves. The proper hour has come. Our country awaits its sons and builders, for its Redemption and yours, for raising its ruins and settling its waste places. Surmount the suffering and travail of the way, because without you Israel will not be redeemed. Delay not, nor lose the proper hour, lest you be late. Dare to go up at once, and do not leave behind you the ancient culture in writing and garb..."

We sold our houses and our possessions without money. We left our synagogues to the gentiles... We came to the synagogues, and we performed a memorial service for the dead, and we read "El Malei Rahamim," and we prayed for pardon and forgiveness, for we knew: The Land of Israel atones for all sins, and our fathers would forgive us. And we took with us on our way the Scrolls of the Law and the holy objects to bring them to our country. And in many places they buried the holy books and Scrolls of the Law in the ground, because they could not take them.

And we prepared provision for the way, every family for itself, dry cakes and boiled butter and dried meat and spices and coffee. And we took with us flour for the way, and the women gathered sticks and baked bread over a tin in the fields, or wrapped the dough about stones and laid them in the fire...

And the boundary was closed to passage because of the multitude of people, and we camped, some here, and some there. And the roads were tumultuous with companies of Jews, and we sat, exceedingly many Jews, about 2,500 together, and we prayed beneath the canopy of heaven... And on the Days of Awe (Rosh Hashanah and Yom Kippur), we prayed exceedingly much, broken-hearted, and weeping on the ground: "When would we merit to enter Israel's gates?"

And there came a day, and the stress of hunger prevailed, and there was no bread for our mouth, And the heart sorrowed for the infants. And we stood and raised our prayers to on High. And the Lord heard our cry, and while we were still praying, Arabs came and brought us food, and said: "Give us money, and you will get bread."

And many of us fell sick on the way, and there was no doctor, and no medicines, and no drop of milk to keep the infants alive. There was only a prayer in our mouth to the Lord that he should help. And many were seized with trembling of the body as though with fever, and yet they walked with us on the way. And there were women near to give birth, and they were on donkeys, and they gave birth while they were riding, and we fulfilled the commandments as was proper, and the woman and child were on the donkey.

And one day a messenger from Israel spoke before us, and strengthened our heart, and filled us with the breath of life, and said to us: "Do not worry. No man will remain in the Exile of Yemen, and the State of Israel will not forsake you. In a little while an end will come to your troubles. There is a Jewish heart in Israel. And you too, let there be no hunger among you." And he fulfilled all his words...

And companies came from all the ends of Yemen, and our heartached in its great yearning for the Land of Israel. And thus we came to Aden as long as there was breath in our nostrils, bruised and robbed, weary and bereft of everything. After a way of travail, sometimes lasting two months and sometimes three, there was not a penny with us nor any possession. Also the rich among us came, most of them without money, in the same position as we, bereft of all. And they gathered us into the great camp which was near the city, and it was on the sands of the desert, and the place was too small for us all, and we lay in large numbers on the sand under the bare sky, next to one another, each family together, and mighty sand-storms raged about us, and in our heart was a prayer for *aliyah,* to fly "on eagles' wings" to our country. And we went up.

Chapter Six

ON EAGLES' WINGS

The actual exodus of the Jews from Yemen was not the result of Zionist propaganda from Israel or elsewhere. Except for a letter received from Jerusalem telling of the setting up of the State of Israel the move was entirely spontaneous on the part of the Yemenite Jews. They had heard, too, that a new David[1] (David Ben-Gurion, first Prime Minister of Israel) now ruled in Jerusalem. When the time came God made them to know that it was time to leave. No other explanation could meet the actual circumstances and facts. Not only did God make them to know that it was time to leave, He put a desire and a determination in them to do so.[2]

The mass move was under way and some were already in the refugee camps in Aden before the authorities in Israel heard of it. As soon, however, as the facts were known an airlift was organized. Large planes, converted bombers, were flown to Aden. They contained only benches, running lengthwise in the plane and thus enabling up to one hundred and thirty of the small, undersized Yemenite Jews to be loaded into one plane. It was all new to the Yemenites. They were a primitive people, entirely unaquainted with machinery or modern scientific development. Only a handful of all the Jews in Yemen had ever seen a plane before, or even an automobile. With considerable trepidation the crew prepared for the first flight from Aden. What would be the reaction of these primitive people? Thousands were to be transported, the first flight would indicate what might be expected.

Slowly men, women and children made their way up the steps, took their places on the benches, sitting cross-legged, and waited in wonder. The crew was wondering, too. The roar of the motors, the movement of the plane, the sudden lifting from the ground, any of these could cause a stampede in the plane. A rush to the door, a crowding of all to one side or an attack upon the crew might wreck the plane. But nothing did happen. Everyone sat quietly, open-mouthed, breathless. Then the plane moved off and was airborne. Soon it was flying smoothly with its strange human cargo. The Yemenites just smiled and explained that God had promised that, ". . . they shall mount up with wings as eagles . . ."[3] Here were the "eagles' wings" provided to bring them back to Zion. Surely it was time for the Messiah to come![4] Maybe He awaited them in Israel!

Altogether 48,000 Jews were flown to Israel from Yemen.

By September 1950 Yemen was empty of Jews. The Magic Carpet could now be rolled up, the eagles could rest. God had spoken and fulfillel His promise. Probably no other prophecy in the Bible has had such an indisputable, unambiguous fulfillment as this phrase "I will say to Yemen, Keep not back."[5] Obviously God has not spoken prior to 1949. Though there had been some who had been able to steal out of Yemen and eventually to reach the Land of Israel, yet their numbers were small and their flight was accomplished with much difficulty. The year 1949 saw the Yemen Jewish population at the highest it had been for centuries, yet by the end of 1950 no Jews were left in Yemen. *This* (the year 1949-1950) unquestionably saw the fulfillment of *that,* (God's promise to Israel through Isaiah 43:6).

Chapter Seven

ISRAEL TODAY

The return of the Yemenite Jews and of those from eastern, western and northern lands has brought great problems to the re-established nation of Israel. Yet each year has seen an improvement in all aspects of life in the new State. Thousands of *dunams* of land have been brought under cultivation and irrigated. Vegetables and fruit are no longer in short supply. Thousands of homes have been built and many new towns and settlements established. The employment situation has improved, many new factories have been built and soon it may be expected that the value of exports will balance import requirements. All this has been accomplished in spite of the Arab economic boycott against Israel. To cap it all, oil is now being produced in Israel to make that land independent of Arab oil supplies, blocked to Israel by Arab enmity and intransigence.

The nineteenth chapter of Isaiah, verses 17 and 18, speak of a war between Israel and Egypt. Here it is written that the Egyptians will be in fear of the Jews and that five cities of Egypt will speak the language of Canaan. If no further conflict ensues, that which took place in November, 1956, already has literally fulfilled this scripture. The Egyptians were in panic when attacked by the Jews. This panic was proved both in Sinai, where Egyptian officers and men fled before the Israeli forces, and on the sea, where an Egyptian destroyer commander had instructions to sink his ship when attacked by an Israeli destroyer (the officers and men were too panic-stricken to do so and the Israel navy captured the Egyptian warship).

Israel soldiers brought back stories of parts of the Sinai desert being littered with shoes. The Egyptian soldiers could run better without them and thousands cast them off and ran barefoot, trying to escape the army of Israel.

Sailors of the Israel navy brought back the story concerning the surrendered Egyptian warship. A leading New York daily paper had a front page story of the scuttling of the Egyptian vessel by her crew. But by then the boat could be seen in drydock in Haifa, having been towed there by an Israeli tug and proving the scuttling story untrue. Most amusing of all was the Arabic news broadcast by Cairo radio heard aboard the ship and which came on just as the boat was towed into Haifa harbor. The news said that Haifa was on fire from end to end as a result of shelling by this destroyer. The truth was that not one shell from this destroyer had landed in Haifa or in any other part of Israel, nor on any Israel vessel.

Five towns in Sinai fell to the Israeli forces and here Hebrew was heard after many centuries of time. The tremendous quantity of military supplies captured there by Israel showed that the Egyptians were indeed terrified of Judah and thought to bolster their courage by heavily arming themselves.

What of the future? Is Israel now firmly established so that she will never again be moved from her land? Has Israel experienced her last exile? What does the Bible say as to the future?

In the Diaspora a great change has taken place in many countries. Several lands which had large-size Jewish populations are now either empty of Jews or contain such small numbers that even synagogues no longer exist.

Thus we see that Isaiah 43:5, 6, concerning the regathering of Israel, cannot be fulfilled at a future date, as far as a considerable portion of it is concerned. The fact that many countries — east, south and north — are now empty of Jews precludes the possibility of a future general regathering. Only by another world-wide scattering from Israel could such a situation be created enabling a future fulfillment of this prophecy. The Bible, however, gives no indication of such a future general dispersal. Yet, even the religious world seems only faintly conscious today of the importance of the re-establishment of Israel and the regathering of the Jews to their own land.

As rapidly as possible Jews from the western part of North Africa are being evacuated to Israel. Egypt has expelled her Jews. Russia must hear the voice of God very soon and release or possibly forcibly eject her Jews. In America and other English-speaking lands Jews will soon feel the 'tug' of the land and join their brethren there.[1] We are at a crucial time in the history of mankind.[2]

Part II

EAST VERSUS WEST—
WILL RUSSIA ATTACK AMERICA?

> And thou shalt come from thy place out of the
> north parts, thou, and many people with thee,
> all of them riding upon horses, a great company,
> and a mighty army.
>
> Ezekiel 38:15

Chapter Eight

The Day in Which We Live

On August 23, 1939, to the consternation of the rest of the world, Hitler concluded a Non-aggression Pact with Russia. As is usual when two unscrupulous dissemblers make an agreement, the contract continued until it suited one of the parties to break it. Then it became but a scrap of paper and was speedily forgotten as Hitler marched his forces east beyond the newly established border of Poland and began his attack on Russia.

Inadvertently Russia was thrown into the camp of those nations eventually allied in war against Hitler. With the full weight of British and American supplies and equipment poured out to Russia and other allies, Hitler was eventually defeated. Hitler's defeat, however, was to require a high price from the Western Powers, for while British and American forces were engaging German forces on the West Front Russia was sweeping westward. It was this westward sweep which brought nearly half of Europe under Communist domination.

With the termination of the war with Hitler a "cold war" began among the victors. This war has been waged now for a number of years, with brief outbreaks into small local "hot wars" in Korea, Indo-China and Vietnam. At the same time Communist so-called "peaceful" penetration into other countries has continued, with complete success in China through revolution, and growing success in India, the Arab states and other Asian countries.

Strangely enough, the resurrection of Russia as a world power and her spreading out to embrace her many satellite countries has been but obedience to the command of God. In Ezekiel 38:7 we read "Be thou prepared, and prepare for thyself, thou, and all thy company that are assembled unto thee, and be thou a guard unto them."

Here are clear instructions from God. It is God's challenge to a God-defying system. They have mocked God, have challenged Him, have defied Him and finally denied that there is a God. God sits in the heavens, manifesting His mercy and grace, for God has no pleasure in the death of the wicked. The time comes, nevertheless, when the cup is full, His wrath overflows and His command goes out, "Prepare!"

The present position of Russia, her power and influence and her satellites gathered under her wing, were thus foretold twenty-five hundred years ago. "Be thou a guard unto them," and down comes the Iron Curtain. It would be difficult to find a more perfect condensation of the story of the rise of Russia.

The rise of Russia must not be thought to result from a superintelligent leadership. Probably at few times in her history of over one thousand years has Russian leadership been at such a low level of intelligence. The answer to the anomaly of this position is found in the next verse of Ezekiel: "After many days thou shalt be visited. . . ."[1] This is a promise from God and in fulfillment of its evil power, a visitation permitted by God has possessed the rulers of Russia. This evil power has given them an abnormal skill and intelligence and enabled Russia to rise to its present height of power. All this was indicated to take place in the "latter years."[2]

Chapter Nine

THE COMMUNIST LINE-UP

In the English translation of the thirty-eighth chapter of Ezekiel, nine proper names are given which have been translated literally from the Hebrew. These are — Gog, Magog, Meshech, Tubal, Gomer, Togarmah, Sheban, Dedan and Tarshish. Three others are given, but in these an attempt has been made to identify them as certain countries of modern times. These three are Persia, Ethiopia and Libya. The literal Hebrew names from which these have been translated are Peres, Cush and Phut. Thus we have twelve names, ten of which appear in the tenth chapter of Genesis. There they are shown to be names of grandsons and great-grandsons of Noah and in verse five of this chapter we are told, "By these were the isles of the Gentiles divided in their lands; every one after his tongue, after their families, in their nations."[1]

These ten were part of the family of Noah which scattered to the ends of the earth. It is possible that after all these descendants had widely separated, the earth was rent apart into the several continents now forming the present earth; Genesis 10:25 might indicate this. The point, however, is irrelevent to the subject. The fact is that Noah's descendants were the progenitors of all the nations on earth. Beginning first as families, they grew into tribes and finally became nations. Though there has been a great shifting of many of these nations, in part or in whole, during the thousands of years since their establishment, and possibly only a small percentage of direct descendants of the original settlers remain in the part of the world originally settled by their earliest fathers, yet this does not affect the value of the names given in Ezekiel. In his prophecy concerning the destruction of Communism he

28

7. Peaceful valleys of Israel to be overrun by troops (a scene in Israel).

8. Rock mountains will crash into the valleys (a scene in Israel).

9. *The Mount of Olives, where Jesus will stand (picture taken from Mount Scopus).*
10. *The Temple Area as seen from the Mount of Olives.*

identified the countries involved by referring to the first settlers after the Flood.

It is known in a general way where each of those mentioned in Ezekiel established themselves. Thus Magog settled well north of Mount Ararat, in what is now Russia. Meshech and Tubal followed and located not far from Magog. Gomer went farther west into what is now Germany and Western Poland. Togarmah settled on the northern slope of Ararat in what was Armenia but is now swallowed up in Soviet Russia. Cush settled in the area which became known as Babylon; Phut (the word literally means "wandering desert tribes") could well be located in the desert between Babylon and Palestine, on the southern fringe of the fertile green crescent which follows the Euphrates and Tigris Rivers.

Sheba and Dedan settled in the southern part of the Arabian peninsula and the port of Aden may preserve the name of its possible founder — Dedan. Tarshish, a grandson of Japheth, the father of the white Gentile races, probably settled in the most western part of Europe and today represents in a general way that part of the world and the English-speaking nations.

There remain two other names. Of these Gog is mentioned as the name of the ruler of the land of Magog. Peres, though not given in the list of descendants of Noah, was the literal name of Persia in Ezekiel's days. Its inconclusion is an exception to the rule Ezekiel was following in this prophecy, probably because that particular part was not settled by any one close descendant by which the land could be identified. The modern name of the land is Iran.

Chapter Ten

IF RUSSIA ATTACKS AMERICA!

There can be no question that for some time the foremost concern in America has been a fear that Russia might attack America. Russia has proved that her own scientific talent, plus her ability through spies and American and British traitors to obtain the secrets of the Western Powers, enables her to more or less keep step with military and scientific development in the West. A Russian lag of six months to a year, or even of two years, behind the Western Powers' military scientific discovery is not important. In the event of Russia attacking the United States she would choose a time favorable to herself, and a time when she would be adequately prepared.

Let us then imagine what might transpire if Russia should attack America tomorrow. Thousands of long-range bombers carrying hydrogen or more powerful bombs would leave Russian bases to converge from east and west on American cities and manufacturing centers. They would span the Atlantic from European satellite and northern Russian airfields. They would fly from Siberian bases through Alaska and northern Canada. Not one, but many air armadas would marshall the existing air strength of Russia in a tremendous surprise "Pearl Harbor" attack, with the aim of wiping out the United States as a major power in the world.

United States and Canadian radar and other listening posts will warn of the danger soon after the planes start. Many of the great Russian bombers will crash in flames as a result of various defense measures. U. S. sonic fighter-planes will meet the armadas far out at sea; self-guided missiles will seek their targets among Russian planes; ground defenses will throw up great defense rings around vital parts and along the coasts. Yet in spite of all defense weapons operating at full strength, there can be little doubt that hundreds of Communist bombers will penetrate to their targets. Bombs, probably many times more powerful than any exploded to this time, will rain down upon New York, Philadelphia, Washington, Detroit, Chicago, Houston, Los Angeles, Seattle and other large cities. No part of the country will escape. One hydrogen bomb landing in the center of a city will wipe a large part of that city off the map. Radio-active clouds will cover the countryside and complete the work of the bombs.

With the present and future development of intercontinental guided-missiles it might even be that long distance bombers as offensive weapons would become outmoded, that all one nation would need to do to destroy another would be to launch a shower of flying bombs with atomic heads upon her enemy. The resultant destruction of a city or manufacturing center would be the same as that accomplished by an immense air-raid, and defense against it would be much more difficult.

One need not draw further on the imagination as to what might happen. Leave out any further destructive elements already in hand or yet to be developed or discovered. Ignore the strength of Russian armies and the fact that from 1950 to 1955 Russia jumped from seventh place as a world naval power to second place. That which exists at present and is pictured above is sufficient to more or less paralyze or destroy the nation and its ability to make war and provide even the necessities of life for its population. It might be centuries before America could rebuild, repopulate and restore the nation to its present standard and strength. Indeed it is doubtful if sufficient heart and ambition would remain in the people to enable them to overcome the destruction all around them.

The picture that has been drawn is not too fantastic. It is well within the bounds of possibility and the reality might be even much worse than has been visualized.

But what of Russia, while the United States is being eliminated as a powerful nation? Knowing such an attack to be momentarily possible a constant twenty-four hour watch is being maintained all around Russia by the Western Powers. It is not without a firm basis of truth that Russia complains she is ringed-in. American and British planes are in a constant state of preparedness. In the event of such an attack by Russia not only would fighter planes be in the air immediately but huge bombers probably in greater number than those of the Communists, would be in the air immediately but huge bombers, probably in would be launched from the United States. The scene we have pictured in America would be duplicated in Russia. Though the country is vaster and distances greater, yet the destruction in populated centers would be as great as in the United States, and Russia too would be immobilized.

Thus both the United States and Russia would be eliminated as to war potential. Only a small fraction of their populations would remain. They would have neither the spirit nor the wherewithal to make war on an extensive scale. If such should be the case (and Russia well knows that this would be the case and therefore restrains herself from an attack on America), then Russia would not be in a position, certainly not for a century, to fulfill the picture of Russian aggression as given in Ezekiel 38. On the basis of this reasoning we do not believe that Russia and the United States will ever war on each other.

Chapter Eleven

The Bible Account of the Russian Attack

Our reasoning as to the possibility of a Russian attack on America has been entirely from a negative standpoint. We pass now to the positive. The Bible clearly pictures a Russian attack, but not on America.[1] It gives roughly the time of the attack, the nations involved and the of the attacking armies. Further, the result of the attack and what will happen to Communist nations is also given. All this is contained in Ezekiel 38 and the first part of chapter 39.

The time comes for God to challenge Russia and its

entire God-defying communistic set-up. "Behold, I am against thee, O Gog... I will bring thee against my land."[2]

The Bible does not indicate so but the writer is of the opinion that Russian military plans will call for an attempt to conquer part or all of the continent of Africa. This vast territory, rich in uranium and gold, contains a great storehouse of many things that Russia needs for her own population. More than that, it contains a great reservoir of man-power to be trained for the Russian armies and factories. At the same time it offers a great base, strategically located outside the Western ring, and provides a stepping-off point to Europe and to South America. If Russia considers that her strength is sufficient to bring into subjection and to control this great area the strategic location of this continent would certainly put her in a position to come close to her dream of world domination.

Furthermore, Russian prospects of Communistic advance into the rest of Asia within the near future present more than a 50-50 possibility. Already China is within the fold, India is drawing near to the day when she will pass behind the Iron Curtain. It is not at all improbable that the Russian bear will swallow up all Asia. In Daniel's vision the bear was commanded to, "Arise, devour much flesh."[3] Thus, with more than half the world population under its control and available for its armies, the possibility of being able to occupy and control Africa would not seem as an unreasonable possibility. In fact the picture would be so attractive that it would appear as the next logical step in conquering the world.

That Israel and the Middle East Arab countries would also offer a rich prize cannot be denied. The great oil deposits of the Arab states now increased by the rich flow of oil in Israel, the wealth of the Dead Sea and other deposits being uncovered by Israel in the Negev desert all add to the prize to be attained. Yet the most valuable feature would be that these countries are an actual land bridge from Europe, through Asia, to Africa.

In a previous chapter it was mentioned that translators of the English Bible had for some unknown reason endeavored to locate the three names in Ezekiel 38:5 as Persia, Ethiopia and Libya. The result has been to completely obscure the information that God wanted to reveal in this verse. Bible students have wasted much time and energy in trying to fit Ethiopia and Libya into the picture. None have succeeded in arriving at a reasonable explanation. One sought to move Libya down to Somaliland to adjoin Ethiopia, and thus at least to get the two countries together, but the result did not clarify the picture. The fact is that neither the land of Ethiopia nor Libya is involved in this prophecy. Peres is definitely Persia, having borne that name from ancient days. Now it is called Iran. Cush settled in what became Babylon, and is now called Iraq.[4] Phut (wandering desert tribes) can well be western Iraq, Syria and Jordan.

A glance at the map (see frontispiece) will show that here is a direct pathway from Russia to the Suez Canal. It is a path that has been used before many times by invading armies from the east: Persia — Iraq — desert — Israel. The prophecy not only indicates the pathway of the Russian forces but also reveals that those in the path will be allied with Russia, joining their forces to those of the Russians. The exception is Israel. She is not to be allied, she is to be the victim. In eleven places in the two chapters of Ezekiel concerned with this prophecy, Israel is mentioned as the place to be attacked.

Equally clear in Ezekiel's prophecy is the approximate timing of the Russian attack. In the latter years, in the latter days,[5] are terms used. Then we are told more definitely—"Into the land (nation) that is brought back . . . and is gathered out of many people . . . to them that are at rest . . . dwelling without walls . . . the people that are gathered out of the nations. . . . In that day when my people of Israel dwelleth safely."[6] Therefore the attack

34

must come after Israel is re-established as a nation, and before the time of "Jacob's trouble."[7]

The setting up of the State of Israel on May 15th, 1948, has clarified much in prophecy and opened windows into the future. Today many future prophetic events, which were confused and unclear ten years ago, are now to be understood in their proper place and perspective. Any book or article explaining future events, written before 1948, is now dated and subject to correction.

The setting up of the State of Israel shows that we are living at a time when Ezekiel 38 is possible of fulfillment. We live in the *last days*. One more event, however, must transpire before the great Russian machine begins to move into the Middle East. It was mentioned in Part One that God would say to the North: *Give up!* It was indicated that over two million Jews living in Russia must be liberated and permitted to go to Israel. Now is the time for the fulfillment of this prophecy.

An inkling of the reaction of the Western Powers to the Russian attack is given in verse thirteen of Ezekiel's passage. *Art thou come to take a spoil? hast thou gathered thy company to take a prey?* One can well imagine activity at the United Nations headquarters and at embassies throughout the Western world.[8] No actual military opposition is indicated. Russia had been encouraged by the policy of the United States at the time of Israel's attack on Egypt some time previous. Russia calls the bluff just as Mussolini and Hitler did decades before, and her great forces roll on uninterrupted.

Chapter Twelve

THE ATTACK

A vivid picture is given of the actual attack of the Russian forces. Through Iran and Iraq the army moves.

Great tanks, mechanized troop carriers, huge guns and all the latest in war equipment move as a mighty wave across the land.[1] Ezekiel describes this as: *All of them riding upon horses.*[2] Here again Bible students have been lead astray by placing the emphasis upon what they are to be mounted on, rather than the fact that they are to be mounted. We have read descriptions of how Russia is buying up horses all over the world and that this is in preparation for the fulfillment of this prophecy. However, the prophet was merely indicating that this great force would be carried, it would not walk on its own feet. Horses were the chief means, in Ezekiel's day, of transport so he used that picture. But the emphasis was on riding, and not on what they rode. It is very doubtful whether there will be a single horse used by the Russian army in this attack.

It had been planned, through an alliance with Egypt, to stockpile vast quantities of war supplies in the Sinai Peninsula. Much had already been stored there when Israel, apprised of the plans in measure and annoyed to distraction by raiding *fedayeen* murder gangs from Egypt, decided on a surprise attack.

The world watched with amazement while the swift-moving army and airforce of Israel penetrated and in less than a week captured the entire Sinai Peninsula. One third of the total Egyptian army was stationed in Sinai. They were armed with the very latest type of Russian weapons and machinery. Yet only a few days were needed for the Israel soldiers to defeat and completely rout the Egyptian forces.

The people of Israel themselves were amazed. They had great pride in their army, airforce and navy, but these forces surpassed anything expected of them. But greater amazement still was expressed at the war booty captured. Only gradually, as the quantities and quality of supplies were revealed was it shown how far advanced were Russian plans for stockpiling in Sinai.

One item found was one *million* heavy wool blankets.

Two other surprise items were two *million* cotton sheets and fifty X-ray machines of latest design. Medicines and the very newest antibiotics were found in sufficient quantity to last Israel for twenty-five years. Fuel oil, gasoline, etc., for the latest type of jet fighters was stored in huge dumps. Trucks, tanks and self-propelled guns of latest design were also part of the booty, together with a complete radar outfit.

Russia made no attempt to hide her chagrin and disappointment at the discovery of her plans and destruction of her supply depots. Probably it was only her preoccupation with events in Hungary that kept her from more active retaliation at that time. However, within a few days new plans were made and Syria was chosen as the new location for the Russian supply base to be prepared for her armies for use in their Middle East advance. The President of Syria came back from a visit to Moscow with an announcement to his people that he had accomplished and received more than he had ever dreamed of, or thought possible.

Then, with everything ready, prophecy begins to unfold further: "Thou shalt ascend and come like a storm, thou shalt be like a cloud to cover the land . . . thou shalt come from thy place out of the north parts, thou, and many people with thee."[3] On and on it rolls, through the Yarmuk Pass, the forces parting here, one going south through the Jordan Valley, the other crossing the Jordan and ascending from the deep north and south rift to the Valley of Esdraelon. Entering this rich valley, it spreads out over valley and mountains alike.

The noise of the advancing force is like a Niagara of sound.[4] The humming and whistling of the jet plane cover, the rattling and clanking of the heavy tanks, the thunderous roaring of the transport motors all blend into a solid wall of sound.

Israel has deployed her small but efficient army in the strongest possible defense points. With full knowledge of the vastness of the forces against her Israel has no illusions as to her ability to stop them but is determined to sell her life dearly. It looks like the end for Israel, but the nation has proved so indestructible and imperishable in the past in spite of repeated attacks and persecutions, that even now hope in God is maintained.[5] The synagogues are full of people praying for the preservation of the nation and right up to the last moment the Foreign Ministry is still trying to influence the Western Powers to come to her aid.

What of the great hydrogen bombs? A country the size of Israel could be almost entirely covered with a dozen or so of such bombs. Why has Russia not smoothed the path before her army and eliminated all opposition by using these monsters of destruction? The answer is that Russian strategy is to keep the Western Powers from coming to the defense of countries she desires to conquer. As long as the penetration is by land forces the danger to the western lands themselves will not appear great. In any case western leaders will hope that the Russian advance will not extend beyond Egypt.

If, however, Russia made a full scale air offensive, dropping hydrogen bombs indiscriminately wherever she chose, the western nations would be alerted and might in turn attack Russia by air. Better to adopt the surer and safer means of gradually swallowing up each country her forces passed through. Let the Powers complain and query. By the time an answer must be made her forces would be established in the great southern continent.

Russian reasoning seemed sound as her armies rolled into Israel, her advance units pushing aside all opposition. Already they had penetrated to the middle of the country, when suddenly, the world around them seemed to erupt.[6] The mountains came tumbling into the valleys burying hundreds of thousands of troops. Great fissures opened in the ground swallowing up men and machines. There followed a tremendous downpour of rain, causing torrents to rush down the mountains still standing and then in overwhelming floods washing all before them in the valleys and pouring on to the sea. Great hailstones began to fall from the skies carrying instant death for all they hit. Then came brimstone, searing and burning. Soon fires broke out on every hand in spite of the floods of water from the skies.

The whole scene was so terrifying and awful that any of the attacking force who survived lost their minds completely and sought to take the lives of their comrades who also survived, then to kill themselves.[7] The destruction of the Communist hordes was complete. "Thou shalt fall upon the mountains of Israel, thou, and all thy bands. . . . So will I make my holy name known in the midst of my people Israel. . . . Thus will I magnify myself, and sanctify myself."[8]

Thus God will meet and deal with the challenge of Communism. Not only on the armies will the wrath of God come, but He also says, "I will send a fire on Magog, and among them that dwell carelessly (godlessly) in the isles."[9] Russia undoubtedly will be eliminated as a world power. With her armies destroyed and destruction in her own land, her war potential will cease. Communism will never be able to rise again.

Chapter Thirteen

WHEN WILL IT BE?

It has been stated already that the time of the fulfillment of Ezekiel's prophecy is to be in the latter days of the latter years. It is to be when Israel has been gathered back to her own land. Further, it is to be at a time when Israel will be at peace and dwelling safely. This latter fact proves that it cannot be at the end of the Tribulation period for the last half of Tribulations will be the time of

Jacob's trouble, when Israel will suffer more than at any time in her history.[1] It cannot be at the beginning or in the middle of Tribulations for we are told that Israel will burn the weapons of war (scrap and melt down the metal of Russian war machines) for seven years following the Russian defeat.[2] Israel will certainly not have an opportunity to burn Russian weapons in the last half of the seven year Tribulation period.

We are thus compelled to believe that Ezekiel 38 must be fulfilled at least three and a half years before the beginning of the seven year Tribulation period.

Considering the matter from the present situation we realize that these events could happen almost at once. The stage is set for this great tragedy and it can happen at any time. The Western Powers have built a great defense wall of NATO powers against Russia. It stretches from Norway in the north, sweeping through Europe to Pakistan in the east. For several years there was a gateway through Iran (Persia) but now that gap has been closed by a makeshift defense organization of several nations. The fact that the two pivotal nations of this group are mentioned by Ezekiel as being allied with Russia in her attack[3] shows how ineffective this new body will be. Certainly this gap will open again and there is no doubt that the two nations — Iran and Iraq (Peres and Cush) will come under Communist control. They will then open the pathway which will lead to the Mountains of Israel.

With everything at this present time so closely approximating the Bible scene as given in Ezekiel, it is almost time for the Lord to move. When will Jesus come for His Church? Will we be taken before Russian forces begin to roll? At the time of their attack? Or after the destruction of the Communist armies and land? We do not know. The Bible does not say. This we do know, these are the last days and Jesus said: "...for in such an hour as ye (the world) think not the Son of man cometh."[4] It behooves all to be ready, prepared and watching, "For the Lord himself shall descend from heaven with a shout, with the voice of the archangel, and with the trump of God: and the dead in Christ shall rise first: Then we which are alive and remain shall be caught up together with them in the clouds, to meet the Lord in the air: and so shall we ever be with the Lord."[5]

PART III

ISRAEL AND THE ANTICHRIST

> . . . he shall exalt himself, and magnify himself
> above every god, and shall speak marvellous
> things against the God of gods, and shall pros-
> per till the indignation be accomplished.
>
> Daniel 11:36

Chapter Fourteen

THE RAPTURE

A hush seemed to rest upon the earth, a breathless air
of expectancy pervaded the atmosphere. Then they were
gone![1] There could be no doubt of it, countless empty places
testified to that fact. Not many in high positions of authority were missing,[2] not many of the wealthy homes had
been disrupted, but among the ordinary folk there were
many empty homes. There were homes too that were
now divided, husbands grieving for missing wives — wives
for husbands.[3] There were many who remained but who
were not ignorant of what had transpired, for they had
been warned but had not heeded.[4]

For some years now unmistakable signs had been in the
earth.[5] In days gone by it had been fashionable to speak
of the coming of the Lord for His Church. Later a
lethargy seemed to overtake those who had lived in mo-
mentary expectation[6] and a spirit of scepticism replaced
watchfulness.

The beginning of Israel's return to her land[7] had
created a stir at first, but so many obstacles seemed to
develop it appeared that after all, this had been premature
and all things still remained as they had been.[8] Yet all
things had not remained as they had been. The Spirit

of God was moving in the earth and suddenly the blue and white flag of Israel appeared — the nation was re-established. Once more Israel dwelt in her own land, a sovereign state. Her exile had ended.

The Jews themselves had not been ignorant of the augury of events. The Yemenite Jews had returned to their ancient homeland expecting the Messiah to be there already. Mr. Ben-Gurion, the first Prime Minister of the State, had said in the Knesset (Parliament) that "...the State of Israel...is the trumpet of Messiah for the in-gathering of the exiles."

Books were written indicating the remarkable sequence of prophetic events which were to be fulfilled in the latter days. A nation had arisen like a phoenix from the ashes of Czarist Russia — a new nation, powerful and defiant. That nation had prepared itself for war whereby it planned to subdue the world and to establish Communism as the world religion and system.[9] Continuing political events and alignment of nations developed just as indicated by Ezekiel[10] and other prophets. Then those Russian hordes were on the march — marching to their doom on the mountains of Israel.

It had all been so accurately foretold by the prophets and correctly interpreted by students of prophecy, that little excuse remained to those who had not prepared themselves. "This is that," could be said in those days with confidence and assurance, and only those who were wilfully blind or uncaring failed to take heed and to make themselves ready.

Now it was all over. The Church had gone — the earth was henceforth unsalted.[11] Russia had accepted God's challenge and gone down to defeat.[12] A new day had dawned for the earth; a new power was soon to unleash itself among the nations.[13] A false millennial Utopia appeared to be on earth's doorstep[14] and the nations were ready to open the door. Faith and spiritual understanding being no longer on earth, deception could be practiced with little fear of detection.[15] Jesus had said, "I am come in my Father's name, and ye receive me not: if another shall come in his own name, him ye will receive."[16]

Chapter Fifteen

The Aftermath

The disappearance of so many from their homes and habitats was a "seven day wonder," but soon became but a memory in the light of rapidly unfolding events. The destruction of the Communist forces in Israel[1] had left an almost insurmountable task to the little nation of Israel. The down-pouring brimstone, the crashing of mountains of rocks into the valleys,[2] the destruction of buildings and homes, the hundreds of thousands of immobilized machines of war, the millions of dead Russian soldiers[3] — all these presented a problem clearly beyond the strength and capacity of Israel to deal with.

Though the people of Israel, including the army, had suffered relatively little in deaths and injuries as compared with the invading forces, yet there had been widespread property damage. The mountains of Judea had experienced the most severe of the earth tremors. In Jerusalem the streets of the business area were full of fallen masonry shaken from the beautiful buildings, many of which had been built since the re-establishment of the State. The great tower of the Y.M.C.A. building had come crashing down into King David Street. Herzl Street was full of debris as was also King George Avenue. The beautiful new buildings of Hakirya, the seat of Israel's government, had stood up well. If it had not been for the fact that most Jerusalem buildings were built of stone from the hills of Judea, few would have stood up under the terrible shaking lasting over a period of hours.[4]

The new buildings of the Hebrew University, west of

44

Rehavia, and the new Hadassah Hospital near Ain Karim had suffered considerably. Millions of dollars would be necessary to repair structural damage and to replace many of the valuable scientific instruments and other equipment.

The Old City, that part of Jerusalem within the ancient walls, had suffered too. Though the walls of the city were solid and little affected, and the vast stones of the Wailing Wall remained unmoved one on top of the other, in the Temple Area, however, a tragedy had occurred. The great cupola of the Dome of the Rock, often erroneously called the Mosque of Omar, had not only split in twain but the beautiful mosaic walls were cracked and rent. Ancient buildings lining the narrow streets had crumbled, in many cases, as though brushed aside by a mighty hand.

On the Mount of Olives the stones of the Russian tower (a landmark on the horizon) tumbled down the hillside and the debris reached to the Garden of Gethsemane. The road to Tel Aviv through the Judean Hills was blocked in many places and the valleys were filled with rocks. On the plains there was little damage from the earthquake, but here the outpoured brimstone, the great hailstones, the rushing torrents of rain which filled every wadi to overflowing, had taken their toll.[5] Grain crops, orange groves, vineyards were washed away or buried under debris. The network of irrigation pipe lines, which carried rivers of water to the southern Negev and up to the Judean hills, were twisted, torn and broken.

Tel Aviv escaped much damage. The Russian troops had not reached within several miles of the outskirts of the city and the outpoured wrath of God was seeking its target among Communist troops. Haifa, too, remained unoccupied by the invading forces, but the severe earth tremors had brought many buildings crashing on the slopes of Carmel.

Every valley in Judea showed the effects of God's

judgment. Every valley, choked with troops the rocks of the falling mountain sides buried, became the grave of millions of black-uniformed Russian soldiers. Dead lay scattered about everywhere; some uncovered, others with parts of their bodies hidden under rocks and earth. Those who had escaped the falling rocks of the mountains, the fire, brimstone and hail, in mortal terror turned upon each other and like drowning men sought to bring their comrades down with them.[6] Now their bodies littered the fields of Sharon and the valleys of the mountains. The Valley of Jezreel, the Jordan Valley and back through the pass of the Yarmuk River (used by invading forces both from east and west from time immemorial), were clogged with bodies of dead Russians. Many months would be required to bury these bodies and to rid the land of the stench of dead and decaying flesh.[7]

It had been amazing how speedily the Russians had moved vast quantities of supplies, instruments of war, tanks, guns and engineering equipment into Israel. Much of this had been stockpiled in Syria after Egypt's defeat by Israel in Sinai. Now immobilized by the destruction of Russian man-power this vast booty presented both a blessing and a curse to Israel. It would take years to break up or utilize all the machines and equipment which encumbered the ground.[8] Yet the scrap iron would provide a large supply of material to aid in reconstruction of their cities and land.

In all its extensive history Israel had never faced greater problems of restoration than now presented themselves. A super-Ben-Gurion was needed. In the early days of the first *Aliyot* (immigration waves) they had had immense problems, but these could be met gradually. The people were then mainly outside the land, in the *Diaspora*, and came in gradually as Halutzim (pioneers) to restore and transform the land. After the victory over the Arabs in 1948 large numbers of immigrants had come and in three and a half years Israel had more than doubled her population. Yet even this inundation did not present the problem that now faced Israel. Clearly help was again needed. No longer was the Zionist Organization available outside Israel to collect vast sums to aid the struggling nation, as had been the case in the forties and fifties. From whence would help now come to enable this nation, which had taken the brunt of the Russian attack, to recover from the terrible destruction it had suffered?

Chapter Sixteen

A NEW WORLD

The elimination of the huge Russian army and the destruction wrought in Russia and its satellite countries[1] meant the termination of Communism as a power or influence in the world. Communist nations were now impotent and never would rise again as world powers. Contrary to the teaching of some Bible teachers, no Russian or Communist soldier would appear at the battle of Armageddon. God's order of judgment was to be: first, the Church, consequent upon its rapture;[2] second, Communism, culminating in its elimination;[3] third, the enemies of natural Israel, culminating in their destruction;[4] fourth, the armies of the nations of the earth, all opposed to God and seeking to remove faith and all evidence of God on earth.[5] This fourth judgment would culminate in the overthrowing of these armies and then the setting-up of Christ's throne on earth.

Nature abhors a vacuum and the disappearance of Communism from the earth left no opposition to the Western Powers. The result was that the desire of many was to be achieved. There was to be one world, ruled over by one ruler. Thus was filled the vacuum in the political world left by the disappearance of Communism.

Feverish war preparations had engrossed the Western

47

Powers for years. The sudden and miraculous defeat of the Russian forces had not been anticipated. A huge defense wall had been built up in Europe, in northern Canada and Alaska. Later, as the movements of the Russian forces indicated Africa to be the first objective of the Communists, defenses in South America and southern Europe drew much attention.

Then, with defense measures at their zenith and hydrogen bombs stacked up in huge supply, came the almost unbelievable news that the Russian army and defense plants had ceased to exist. Without the Western Powers firing a gun or dropping one bomb, the enemy of world freedom had been wiped out. It was too good to be true, there must be some mistake. Yet the news continued to pour in by press dispatches, radio and television. Soon every television and cinema screen revealed pictures of the dead army of Russia, the fallen mountains and destruction in Israel. Communist authority in their own lands was now so paralyzed that reporters and photographers roamed at will behind the "Iron Curtain" and kept the newspapers turning out frequent special editions with their stories and pictures.

A few gave God the glory for this delivery from what had been a nightmare of fear. Any reasonable person would have realized that such a deliverance could be accomplished only by God. This, however, was not a reasonable age. It had become an age of "man-worship," since formal Christianity had ceased to be a religion of worship of Jehovah God. As a result, the world wanted to worship a man and to give him credit and praise for the peaceful conditions now existing.[6]

The United Nations continued to function and delegates from Communist countries continued to sit in the General Assembly, the Security Council and in other committees of that body. Yet, gradually, it became evident that a change was taking place in the world government.

The United States, as the leading power, began more and more to assert herself. As leader of the nation the President became the recognized world leader and drew to himself the adoration and worship of the other nations. Others, however, had striven for centuries for such authority and rule and were not prepared now to surrender their ambitions and behind-the-scene scheming.

Centuries earlier Romanism had suffered a severe defeat in England. In France, Germany and other countries its power had been seriously challenged. The United States of America had its beginning in a Protestant demand for freedom of worship and with its development became the largest Protestant country. However, Rome gradually enlarged its position and forces there. Immigration was organized from countries predominately Roman Catholic and large families were encouraged by the "Holy Father." In every way possible the ranks of Romanism were enlarged and their position strengthened. Political lobbying went on night and day with one object only in mind, that of eventually gaining control of the government of the United States of America. In America much had been said and written against Communistic plans and efforts to attain world control, yet Rome had striven for this same thing for centuries before Communism had been introduced.

Relentlessly through the years Rome sought to advance its cause. In America it was approaching that goal much more rapidly than most people realized. Gradually the complexion of the House of Representatives and the Senate changed until a Roman Catholic majority was in control in both houses. Labor had made a supreme effort to gain the upper hand politically but had failed, due to the fact that Romanism had used it as a ladder in its own upward climb. Now, with the installation of a Roman Catholic president, the goal was reached. Rapidly all important positions in government were filled by henchmen of Rome. In this way the age old dream was realized. Scripture was fulfilled, for the woman arrayed in purple and scarlet and decked with gold and precious stones now sat upon the scarlet colored beast. Rome was solidly in control of the government of the United States of America, and hence the recognized world head.[7] Soon the seven heads and ten horns of the beast were to appear. Apostate Protestantism and other religious bodies came into line and all Christianity was under one head, who had both secular and religious authority throughout the earth.

All opposition to the world authority had been smothered, so wars ceased and an era of peace was inaugurated unlike anything the world had ever seen before. No longer was there a desperate race between the nations to accumulate armaments, giant bombers, navies and other means of destruction. All the war factories and shipyards, all the scientific laboratories and experimental stations, all the millions of men in the armed forces were now released for civilian production and discovery. Whereas men had striven previously to make larger and more destructive bombs, they now engaged their scientific minds and experience in tackling the everyday problems of life. Whereas scientists formerly endeavored to create faster surface ships and submarines to outrange the enemy, more deadly guided missiles of offense and elaborate defense set-ups to stop enemy planes, etc., now these brains were devoted to creating a world in which it would be easier to live.

Attempts were made to solve problems such as overcrowding in cities, relief of traffic congestion, danger to life on the highways, safety devices for aircraft, streamlining of educational methods so as to do away with slipshod and incorrect teaching in schools and universities, proper utilization of machinery so as to enable man to earn more and work less. All these weaknesses of civilization, and many others were considered and solutions found. The problem of overpopulation and undersupply of foodstuffs was solved by regulation of family life and improved distribution methods. All the deadly diseases of mankind were conquered. This era gradually assumed the characteristics of the Millennium, with peace on earth, law and order established everywhere and prosperity for all.

This was truly a Utopia. Men looked back to the times under the old system when ambitions of the nations, differences between capital and labor and ravages of disease and poverty made life burdensome and difficult. What a different picture conditions now revealed. The storms of nature had been controlled in part; there was employment for all under ideal conditions. Living conditions for all were raised to a high standard. Educational facilities were available for young and old which developed the minds of all to a high level. Little wonder that the world honored and obeyed the man who was given credit for bringing all this about.[8]

The United Nations Organization had ceased to exist as such. There was now one world leader and a super world cabinet. This council had been formed to take over all activities of the former U.N.O. with this difference: it had force to back up its decisions. All authority was now in the hands of the President and he delegated this as he wished to his council. The council consisted of seven ecclesiastical leaders and ten secular leaders.[9] The seven were former cardinals of Rome. The office of Pope no longer existed, all the former power and authority of this position now rested in the President. He was infallible both in religious and secular affairs. The seven cardinals had complete control over all religious matters in every country and all religions had been unified. The only exceptions to this were the Jewish and Moslem religions. Members of these two religions were permitted to observe their form of worship, with certain reservations, but could not receive converts.

The ten secular leaders were individually dictators in their respective countries, subject always to instructions from the President. They had control over all affairs of state in all countries. The combined council, with the President (himself a former cardinal) at its head, ruled the world. The President had for many years been a popular TV figure. His appearances had been watched with interest and admiration, not only by Roman Catholics but also by Protestants. His smooth glib speech, his bright piercing eyes, his long flowing robes had all combined to win him a great following of admirers.

Religious worship was on an entirely new basis. Except for Jews and Moslems there was only the one religion in the world. Everyone was compelled to attend at least one service each week. There was a slight resemblance to the former Roman form of worship but the President was worshiped as God,[10] and all hymns were in praise of him. The Bible was not used,[11] nor were people permitted to have copies of this book in their homes. In place of it a new "Bible," based on philosophy, and setting forth the perfect way of life for each day, had been published. It contained in addition a catechism to be used for moral and religious instruction, a statement of doctrine and faith, information on a practical application of the suggested principles for everyday living and a long dissertation by the President setting forth the superiority and advantages of the new religion,[12] as contrasted with the former religions of superstition and tradition.

Chapter Seventeen

THE MIDDLE EAST SITUATION

Though the feverish race for armaments and instruments of destruction was ended, there remained the question of policing the world. A vast World Police force had been organized and large units of these police were stationed at strategic points, ready to be rushed at a moment's notice to any spot where trouble might threaten.

The Middle East remained as one of the most combustible points. Both the Jewish and Moslem religions were permitted to continue. The Moslems constituted a vast body, though not a closely knit group. They numbered more than five hundred million in the world but were scattered across North Africa, the Middle East, Pakistan, Southeast Asia and China. As members of so many different nations they could not present a united force, yet the vastness of their numbers made them a power to be reckoned with. Recognizing this, the President permitted them to continue their worship of Allah, but required at the same time a token recognition of himself as the earthly leader.

Many were surprised when it was announced that Judaism would be permitted to continue and that Jews could worship their God in their own way. The reason for this favor was not evident. The ruling had come directly from the President himself, overriding the advice of his religious council. For some reason the world ruler seemed to desire to cultivate Jewish goodwill and friendship.

* * * * * * * * *

The destruction in Israel required almost a superhuman effort to restore the land that it might become productive

53

once more and a fit country in which to live. The first problem had been the bodies of dead Russian soldiers. A special place for burial had been chosen where there was considerable depth of earth.[1] Giant bulldozers and mechanical shovels worked night and day digging out mass graves. Though all citizens were conscripted, seven months were required to complete this unsavory task.[2] Then had begun the attempt by the people of Israel to restore some order out of the chaos. The task was enough to discourage the most stouthearted. The streets of Jerusalem first received attention. No attempt could be made, as yet, to rebuild. It was sufficient for the time being if the debris could be cleared away. Broken water pipes to the Negev and other waterlines were a first priority, too. As leaders planned and men worked it seemed a hopeless task. Despair all but engulfed the people. Food was short and few factories could produce for export to relieve the desperate economic situation. Tremendous piles of scrap iron began to accumulate as the Russian war machines were broken up.[3] The export of this scrap material helped a little but still left a tremendous gap between the export figure and that required for imports of the bare necessities. Israel struggled on for several years and, though some cities began to resume their former appearance in a measure, the task seemed to become more impossible as the years went by.

This was the situation when the new President took office. He had been an American cardinal and now took over the office which put him in the position of world ruler. None would have expected that such a mild-mannered, studious, smooth-tongued priest would have risen to such a position of eminence. Those, however, who had had dealings with him knew something of his iron will. They had seen a cruel glint in his bright eyes and had detected a note of cynicism in many of his utterances. In some respects he appeared as a sinister figure and there were those who knew something of the ruthless methods he had used to come into power.[4]

Shortly after assuming office the President called the leaders of Israel — the Chief Rabbis of Jerusalem, the Prime Minister, the Minister of Foreign Affairs and the Minister of Finance — to a conference in Washington. The matters discussed were not made public but it was learned that a secret agreement had been entered into between the World Authority and the Government and Rabbinate of Israel. Rumor was that Israel had signed a seven year contract.[5] This was to guarantee Israel sufficient funds to restore her land to its original condition of productivity, both agriculturally and commercially. Much more than this, however, was the rumor (as yet only spoken in a whisper among the Jews), that the Temple Area was to be given to Israel and funds furnished to build a magnificent temple outshining any previous temple or any building in the world. What Israel was to give in return for all this was not yet clear. What had Israel to offer for such munificence?

Chapter Eighteen

JERUSALEM

Restoration took on a new lease of life in Israel. Huge dirt moving machines, great bulldozers and other machinery were soon on the job completely restoring the land. Huge rocks were pushed to one side revealing rich earth underneath. Once more the valleys began to present beautiful vistas as farms dotted their length. Where a short time before there had been nothing but piles of rock, broken machines and ruins of towns and *kibbutzim* (settlements), there now rose attractive modern villages and beautiful individual and collective farms. Irrigation pipes were relaid and the earth again produced rich green crops. In the Sharon citrus trees were planted, sufficient to literally "fill the face of the world with fruit."[1] In the industrial areas, nearby Haifa and Tel Aviv, factories were restored or rebuilt on the most modern pattern and equipped with the latest types of machinery.

The southern part of Israel, the vast Negev desert, had been partly developed before the Russian attack. Negev settlements and farms had not suffered greatly in the disaster that swept over Israel, but the disruption of the irrigation systems and the cessation of the flow of water had left parched fields and dying trees. Some effort had been made to restore the previous settlements but the shortage of water limited progress and little had been accomplished. Soon the benefits accruing from the new agreement with the World Leader were apparent in the desert, too. The limitless amounts of money provided for Israel enabled not only the restoration of the old desert settlements but a new development on a scale scarcely dreamed of in the early days of the State. Now the desert was literally blossoming as a rose.[2] Huge crops (in many cases three and four in one year) were raised by constantly irrigating and fertilizing the rich, sandy soil. Nowhere in the world did vegetables and fruit grow so large and so choice as in the Negev of Israel.

As the months went by Jerusalem became aware of activity on the former Temple Area. Solomon's Temple had stood there thousands of years ago, but since the destruction of Herod's Temple in 70 A.D. by the Romans under Titus, no Jewish building had occupied this site. Since the occupation of Jerusalem by the Moslems in 637 A.D. the former Temple Area had been considered a "Holy Place." Next to Mecca and Medina, Jerusalem was the third most holy site in the world to Mohammedans. However, the activity observed was not that of Moslems. Only Jews were seen now on this site, where formerly they had been forbidden and where it had meant instant death for any Jews to enter.

Then the story broke. It was a seven-day wonder and papers all over the world revealed details of the secret agreement made between the President and the Jews.[3] The Temple Area was to be made available to the Jews on which to build once again a temple for the worship of Jehovah. Moslem leaders had been secretly in formed by personal representatives of the World Ruler. There had been no public outcry for the Moslems had been told that for them it was a case of give up the *Haram Esh-Sherif* or Islam would cease as a permitted religion. There was no doubt that the Leader was able to enforce such an ultimatum and to eliminate this religion from the face of the earth. It was clear that the President was favoring the Jews and seemingly could not do enough for them. Yet why this should be was still a mystery to the world, and to the Jews. What had the Jews to offer to pay for all these favors and help?

Some years were to pass before the Temple would be completely finished and shine in all its glory. This, however, would not hinder the restoration of worship at an early date. Work was ordered so that the central part of the Temple would be rushed to a degree of completion which would enable services to be held and the priests to officiate. The great altar also was to be erected at once and the laver. The choosing of the High Priest was to be made an event of outstanding importance in the history of Israel. Several coveted this office, especially the whitebearded Chief Rabbi of Jerusalem. There was considerable discussion in the various rabbinates as to the method to be used for choosing the High Priest. Some Talmudic students favored a vote only of those subscribing to the Agudah Israel school. Others favored a vote by all rabbis. Still others felt that all Jews should vote in a democratic manner to choose the religious leader of their people. Jewish political leaders were apprehensive of a curtailment of their authority and wished to limit the power of the High Priest.

At the height of the discussion a messenger arrived from Washington. He bore a dispatch from the President to the Jewish leaders informing them that the President had himself chosen the High Priest and that Joshua Ben-Elohainu was appointed to that office. Further, the President commanded, the High Priest would be recognized as the supreme authority in Jewry and the State would be subject to his rule. There were bitter thoughts and gnashing of teeth among Jewish leaders but none dared open their mouths nor say a word against the appointment.

Joshua Ben-Elohainu was known as a man of great learning and influence in Israel. He was born in Jerusalem and was fifty years of age. Educated in Jerusalem in the Hebrew University and Talmudic institutes he had acquired a tremendous grasp of Jewish history and Talmudic learning. In later years, through various special courses abroad, he had rounded out his education and had become a famous author. He was known as a temperate man who lived an almost monastic life. No better choice could have been made for a leader in Israel and, except for those with personal ambitions, the choice was popular in Jewry.

With the appointment of the High Priest the whole set-up of government was changed and put on a theocratic basis. The High Priest was supreme and in a short time had organized both the secular ruling authority and the priesthood. Israel was fortunate in the choice that had been made for its leader. Another man might have ruled with a cruel iron hand. Joshua, however, showed himself to be a humble leader anxious to do the best for his people.

The last Jewish sacrifice had been made three weeks before the Temple had been destroyed in 70 A.D. Jerusalem had been besieged at the time by the Romans and finally all the sacrificial animals had been slain and no further living animals were available. The priests had carried on the Temple worship without sacrifices for another three weeks. Then, on the ninth of Ab, the inner walls of the city fell; the Temple was desecrated and destroyed and there had been neither temple nor sacrifice since that day nearly two thousand years ago.[4]

It was decided that the daily sacrifices must be renewed at the earliest possible moment. Work was rushed on the Temple and plans made so that the services would begin and the first sacrifice slain on the anniversary of that date in 70 A.D., when the sacrifices had ceased. This was to be a day both of mourning and rejoicing. Mourning for 1900 years of suffering and exile; mourning for the destruction of the Temple and 1900 years away from God. Their prophet had written, "For the children of Israel shall abide many days without a king, and without a prince, and without a sacrifice. . . . Afterward shall the children of Israel return, and seek the Lord their God, and David their King. . . ."[5] Now the clock had turned full circle and God had restored to them, ". . .beauty for ashes, the oil of joy for mourning. . ."[6] So they would rejoice as they came back to God and once more would offer a blood-sacrifice for sin as commanded in the Torah.

As the day for the renewal of Temple service and sacrifices drew near, people poured into Jerusalem from all parts of the world. The President was unable to attend but a vast television screen had been prepared on the front of the Temple building, and with the development of world television relay in recent years, his image, as he spoke in Washington, would appear on the screen.

This new development was called *Rayscreen*. The relay was produced by reflecting rays back and forth from earth stations to satellites suspended five hundred miles above the earth. In this way the globe could be encircled in any direction. Hundreds of thousands of people would face the screen in Jerusalem and see the World Leader and hear him speak.

The day dawned bright and clear. Hours before, people had begun to assemble in the Temple courtyard. At dawn the first sacrificial lamb was led out to the altar. The knife of the priest flashed, smoke began to rise from under the altar and the sacrifice was consumed in the flames. Suddenly the sky darkened, a most unusual phenomenon at that time of year. Lightning flashed from one end of the heavens to the other, accompanied by peal after peal of deafening thunder. Then came a downpour of rain which threatened to wash away sacrifice, altar, priests and the great concourse of people. The storm was over in ten minutes but the sky remained dark and the sun did not appear again that day. People asked one another, "What did this portend? Was God displeased?"

At seven in the morning (midnight in Washington) the face of the President appeared on the great screen. A smile lighted up his face, but his words were like steel bullets pouring forth from the many loud-speakers.

"High Priest, leaders and citizens of Israel, visitors in Jerusalem," he orated. "On this day which is outstanding in the history of Israel I offer my congratulations to a nation revived, restored and rebuilt in its land after an absence of 1900 years. It has been my pleasure to help restore both your land and your Temple.

"On this occasion of the restoration of your Temple worship it is well to remember that this site was chosen by your God as His dwelling place on earth.[7] Here you worshiped and sacrificed to your God. Here your God put His Name and accepted your worship.[8] Here I have permitted and enabled you to rebuild your Temple and to worship. I have kept my word. I have fulfilled my covenant. I will continue to be your protector and herewith command you to worship in this Temple. I have spoken."

The cheers which followed the brief and abrupt speech of the President were given dutifully, in view of the presence of many high representatives of the President and hundreds of secret police ever ready to report any lack of enthusiasm for the World Leader. However, most of those present sincerely rejoiced, believing that the God of Israel would be pleased with the renewal of Israel's sacrifices on the Temple altar, and would henceforth smile on their nation.

In spite of the beauty and richness of the great buildings there was one thing lacking. Israel sensed this lack and wondered — there was no glory cloud, no feeling of God in their midst. Where was God? Was their return to temple worship and sacrifices not pleasing to Him? "Oh God of Abraham, Isaac and Jacob, bless Your people and Your Temple. We have wandered nineteen hundred years. We are weary and tired of our wandering and would solace our souls once more in Your presence. Return, Oh God, and bless Your people Israel! Speak again, and Your servants will hear and answer."

Chapter Nineteen

Rending the Veil

Three and one half years had passed since the renewal of temple worship. Israel, by now, was accustomed to the form of worship. The smoke and fire of the altar, the bleating and bellowing of the sacrifice animals and the

61

daily ministration of the priests had become almost commonplace to the Jews. For the last few months, however, there had been some strange foreign activity in the Temple courtyard which no one seemed to be able to explain.

It had started shortly after the receipt of a note by Joshua Ben-Elohainu, which came from the President. The note had informed the High Priest that certain construction work would be undertaken in a small area of the Temple courtyard. The work was to be done by workmen sent from America, who would require no assistance from the Jews but must be permitted to work unhindered. Work would be suspended on Saturdays and Sundays.

The workmen arrived and began to construct a tall wooden structure, one hundred feet square and a hundred fifty feet high. All material had been brought on their ship and moved to the site in closed trucks of great size. All the workers were close-mouthed and kept entirely to themselves. They never entered into conversation with any of the Jews, and from the beginning the construction work had been guarded night and day by a large force of World Police, changed and replaced every three days. None were permitted to approach near the hastily built building. Some, however, had said that they had heard the sound of hammers on stone coming from within the building.

Eventually it became evident that a new stage had been reached in the work. The rough covering forming the building was now being dismantled board by board. Within could be seen a small building or covered object. When all the wooden framework was removed there remained what appeared as a steel frame of four uprights encircled by iron loops. The actual frame could only be conjectured at, for it was covered and almost concealed by a rich tapestry covering. Not the slightest hint was offered as to what was inside this queer tent like structure.

*　*　*　*　*　*　*　*　*

Prosperity had come to Israel. The rebuilt factories were working night and day to fill export orders for the multitudinous items now manufactured in the land. Hundreds of thousands of *dunams* of land were planted with citrus trees. The replanting had given employment to thousands and soon Israel would be filling the face of the world with fruit.[1] No other oranges compared with those grown in Israel. Land had been brought under citrus cultivation which only a short time before had been desert. When blossom-time came in January and February the desert not only blossomed "as a rose," but was perfumed more fragrantly than any rose garden.

Uranium from the Negev now provided raw material for the huge converters which provided sufficient power for all Middle East electrical requirements. Indeed, Israel was close to leadership in world nuclear developments through her scientific institutes which were staffed by some of the ablest scientists of the world, worthy successors of Einstein and his contemporaries.

In medical development Israel had already outstripped the rest of the world. Hadassah Medical Institute in Jerusalem and its affiliated colleges and research laboratories had produced cures for practically all human ailments previously considered incurable. Israel was no longer an insignificant nation, for now it was recognized and appreciated for the excellence of its products, the extent of its scientific discovery and its high standard of culture and education.

Jerusalem, Tel Aviv and other cities and villages were enjoying the end of their Sabbath. As usual the main streets of the cities were thronged with strolling couples and groups of Jews dressed in their Sabbath clothes and filling both sidewalks and roadways and making it

63

almost impossible for cars to push their way through. They were gay happy throngs, all well-clothed and prosperous looking.

Not only prosperity but peace had finally come and it seemed as though the "controversy of Zion"[2] was ended. Sabbath was surely a time when all Israel could show its enjoyment of its new freedom and liberty. The future outlook was bright, even beyond the dreams of the early Zionist "dreamers." This night was much as other end-of-Sabbath nights, until a trumpet suddenly sounded through the streets. The blast had come from the loud-speakers put up at strategic points in all cities, villages and *kibbutzim* throughout the country. It indicated a special message to be issued from World Headquarters in Washington. First the message would be given in English, immediately followed by a Hebrew translation.

The laughing, moving throngs became tense, rigid, as words began to pour forth. All gathered as close as possible to the many speakers and hung on every word.

The message stated that next Sabbath, at twelve noon, an event of outstanding importance would take place in the Temple Area in Jerusalem. The President himself was flying to Israel to take part and to make a personal announcement at that time. All Jews that could be accommodated in Jerusalem were to proceed there immediately for this event. The message was repeated every hour through the night and next day, so that none could be ignorant of its content. It brought amazement and wonderment in Israel and was a headline story in the world press. What could it be? What could be so important to bring the great World Leader to Jerusalem? Not only in Jerusalem, but throughout the world people discussed the announcement and what it presaged.

Friday afternoon, well before the beginning of Sabbath, the great private air-saucer arrived carrying the most important man in the world and his closest associates. There followed ship after ship carrying the entire inner council of the seven cardinals, their deputies, secretaries, specialists and armed escort. Their saucer ships darkened the skies, then seemed as giant flies on the immense new airfield constructed on a large, elevated plateau.

The great atom-powered saucer ships were two hundred feet in diameter. They actually seemed as two saucers with their rims together, one upside down on the other. They were powered with four power plants producing repellant rays which forced the ship directly upward until height was attained, and then in a horizontal direction. The ships were capable of traveling at speeds up to one thousand miles an hour vertically and two thousand five hundred miles an hour horizontally. They could hover in the air without vertical or horizontal motion.

Millions of cubic meters of rock and earth (thrown down mountains)[3] cleared from the nearby valleys had been moved to build up the tremendous airport. It was one of the largest and best equipped in the world, with sections for airliners, another for private planes, and the largest of all — that which was used as a base for the strategic air police. This was Base Three, recognized as one of the most important in all the ring of air bases around the world. It was at this base that the President and his party landed.

From the airport a super ten-lane three-level highway had been built through the mountains to Jerusalem. Soon a fleet of atom-powered six-wheelers, sleek and powerful, streaked along the thruway at a speed of one hundred and fifty miles an hour. In a few minutes the leading car drew up before the beautiful Utopia Hotel in Jerusalem. There, in the magnificent President's suite, the leader of the world made his headquarters. The hotel itself was entirely requisitioned for the use of the Presidential party and the security personnel.

Jerusalem was full of visitors. It seemed as though almost every Jew in Israel had come to Jerusalem in obedience to the summons. The Sabbath morning sacrifice service in the Temple had been unusually solemn and impressive, and had been attended by an immense throng. Every religious and secular leader in Israel of any standing at all had received special instructions relative to the Sabbath. By eleven A.M. each was to be seated in the seat specially reserved for him in the immense stands which had been erected speedily in the Temple Area. These stands had been built in a semi-circle facing east. They looked directly towards the great tower, tapestry-covered, which had recently been erected with so much secrecy as to its content and purpose. Thousands of others received gate-passes to the Temple Area, entitling them to standing-room in front of the stands or on the east side. All others would have to find vantage points on the walls and the surrounding buildings, or on the Mount of Olives and Mount Scopus.

Long before daylight people began pouring into the Temple Area and toward the Mount of Olives. Indeed, many had spent all night on the hillside for want of a better place to stay, or in order to obtain a vantage point for the morrow. By eleven A.M. the hillsides were black with a tremendous mass of people. On the city walls and on every building which offered a view of the Temple Area people seemed to cling like flies. The stands in front of the Temple were full to capacity, and except for the carpeted path from the main gateway to a platform in front of the high tower, it seemed as though every inch of standing-room was occupied. On a special platform between the tower and the stands the High Priest, Joshua Ben-Elohainu, the Chief Priests of the Temple and secular leaders of Israel were seated. A special section of the stands had been reserved for the priests and officers of the Temple, while lesser officials and servants found good points to view the proceedings from the upper parts, even to the pinnacle of the Temple building.

Everywhere in the stands, on all parts of the Temple Area and even to the crest of the Mount of Olives uniformed special units of the World Police stood smartly at attention. Surrounding the tower were drawn up in a huge circle one thousand of the specially selected and trained President's Bodyguard. They faced outward toward the people, with their backs to the tower. In their crimson and green uniforms, their brightly shining helmets and chromed ray guns, they were the acme of precision and smartness.

At eleven forty-five a thirty-gun salute began to be fired at twenty second intervals from the hill in front of the former United Nations Headquarters, the buildings of which had originally been built by the Mandatory power of Palestine for the High Commissioner.

While the salute was being fired a further one thousand members of the special Bodyguard marched in smartly in two ranks. Arriving at the base of the platform the heads of the two columns parted, circling the base on both sides until their leading men reached the ranks of their comrades surrounding the tower. At a word of command the two columns halted and turned inward facing each other. A further command and the ranks stepped back smartly until each rank was standing on the edge of the long purple carpet. With their ranks closed up they made a wall of five hundred men on each side of the carpet, from the gateway to and around the platform.

Exactly on the dot of twelve a tremendous blast from one hundred trumpets heralded the arrival of the President. As he slowly proceeded along the carpeted way every eye was upon him. At least two million people watched him reach the steps and ascend to the platform. On the platform a large golden throne had been placed and the President, the ruler of the world, seated himself. He presented a picture of medieval grandeur. His mitre was made of pure gold, studded with many diamonds which glittered in the bright sun. He was dressed in robes of gold and purple and a beautiful white ermine cape covered his shoulders. Nothing more lavish could be imagined. Those who had caught a glimpse of his shoes under his purple robe claimed that they were of the finest leather covered with pure gold scales overlapping each other like those of a fish. In his hand was a staff five feet long, plated thickly with pure gold and crowned on the top with a single real diamond five inches in diameter, the largest diamond ever found.

Following the President, at a distance of fifty paces, the seven cardinals had come in, two by two, with the seventh bringing up the rear. They too presented a dazzling sight, with pure white robes almost hidden under crimson dyed capes of beautiful marten fur. On their heads were golden framed headpieces covered with Russian sable dyed crimson to match their capes. They too ascended the platform and took their seats in a semicircle facing, and at the foot of, the throne.

Then came a brilliant array of ecclesiastics and representatives of all nations. The head of this column stopped at the foot of the steps to the platform and remained standing facing the President, while the long column of dignitaries closed ranks until they too presented a great mass of faces as they stood on the carpeted pathway between the two ranks of Bodyguard troops.

Thus was arrayed the greatest pageant the world had ever witnessed. There was an element of mystery to it all, for only a few knew what was to follow. The plans and preparations had been executed with such secrecy that not a whisper had reached the ears of any except those involved in the work. Now the stage was prepared.

The setting was magnificent, with the great Temple building, its golden roof shining in the bright sun, as a background, and the vast concourse of people crowding almost every inch of space in the courtyard, on the walls and buildings and on the Mount of Olives. The bright colored robes of the chief participants and leaders were as brilliant jewels in a massive setting. Dominating all was the beautifully tapestried tower, before which the President sat on his throne. The covering of the tower was woven in brilliant colors forming most extraordinary patterns. Four scenes were depicted on this tapestry. One was of fiery red serpents crawling out of a pit. The second was a beast of most unusual ferociousness, its right paw lying heavily on a prostrate human form. The third depicted a huge golden image of a man, the face vaguely familiar to those able to see it from their positions, and the fourth showed the figure six, appearing three times,[4] each figure entwined with the other, giving the appearance of a chain hanging down the tapestry. The figures were in gold on purple.

Sufficient loud-speakers had been placed at various points so that every single person forming part of this amazing spectacle, whether in the Temple Area or outside, could hear every word of the address about to be given by the World Leader. In fact, the whole proceedings had a world coverage on television (or Rayscreen) so that not only the President's voice was heard, but he himself was seen. No accurate count could be made of those who actually saw and heard the proceedings, but possibly around one billion people viewed it and heard the words of the speech.

Rising slowly, as every eye watched and every tongue was stilled, the President stood to his feet. His raised hand may have been a gesture of salutation or a demand for silence. If the latter, it was unnecessary, for the air seemed hushed and still awaiting the revelation to come.

"My people," the leader began, "this day is unique in the history of man. You are gathered before me in this city of Jerusalem or you view me on your Rayscreens. You are gathered at my command. I speak to all people but my remarks apply specifically to those of the Jewish religion.

"It was on this site, at the command of your God, that your father King David prepared for the erection of your first temple.[5] This temple was erected by King Solomon and in it you worshiped your God, Jehovah. You believed that your God dwelt in this temple and your Bible claims that He supernaturally revealed His presence at the time of its dedication.[6]

"And now, after nineteen hundred years, I have graciously permitted you to once more worship your God in this newly erected temple which I enabled you to build. I have restrained all opposition, and have restored to you opportunity for worship as it existed when your fathers dwelt in this land and possessed all authority.

"For three and a half years you have worshiped your God according to your ancient rites and laws. Now the time has come for you to be enlightened and you will know why I have sponsored the reorganization of your temple worship and sacrifices. Give honor to whom honor is due. In years gone by your God was not able to maintain His residence in the temple nor to protect it from destruction by His enemies.[7] Your God could not protect you as you were forced to flee from your land and to serve nineteen hundred years in bondage.[8] Your God could not enable you to build your temple again, BUT I DID!

"Let all the world behold!"

At this cry the great tapestries covering the high tower slowly parted at the front and gathered together at the back of the metal frame. Then was disclosed to all eyes a huge stone image one hundred feet high. It was an image of the President, a perfect likeness, standing with arms folded and a sardonic smile on the face. Suddenly, while the people gazed with mingled feelings of awe, fear and admiration, the image began to speak.[9]

"Men and women of the earth: For millenniums of time, since you first lived on this earth, you have worshiped gods. In your ignorance you have worshiped gods many, or god singular, yet you have not known *me*.

"Today, I have chosen to reveal myself. This day is the most important in all the history of man. This day I am opening your eyes and permitting you to see and to acclaim the true God. I AM GOD! WORSHIP ME! I AM THE CREATOR! I MADE HEAVEN, I MADE EARTH. THERE IS NO GOD BESIDE ME.[10] SEE MY POWER!"

Suddenly the sky was rent, a great pillar of fire flashed down and rested upon the dome of the Temple.[11] The earth trembled and rocked.

Then the image continued to speak:

"Henceforth you will worship me as God. You will bow down to me. You will be marked with my mark and everyone who fails to bow to me and to receive my mark will be ostracized from society. You will not be able to purchase the necessities of life, you will not be able to sell your time or produce.[12] You will die the death which I have ordained.[13]

"Israel — I am your true God. You have ignorantly worshiped your false god-Jehovah but now I have opened your eyes. For this purpose I enabled you to erect your temple and to restore worship as in the days of your fathers. Now I COMMAND YOU TO WORSHIP ME — I AM GOD, WORSHIP ME!"

His closing words ended on such a high pitch as to be almost a screech.

Chapter Twenty

To Your Tents!

During the whole period of the speech and the demonstration of fire from heaven, the assembled multitude had stood as though turned to stone. With the final exultant scream of the stone image demanding worship the spell was broken. On every hand Jews began to cry and to lament and suddenly a voice shrieked over the loud speakers. It was the voice of Joshua Ben-Elohainu, the High Priest. He had forced his way to the President's platform in the confusion which followed the speech. Shoving all aside he seized the microphone.

"People of Israel," he cried, "to your tents! What part has Israel in idols and false gods? Flee to your hiding place. This man is evil, this power is of Satan, he is the great deceiver, be not deceiv. . . ."

The voice died abruptly in a choked sound. With a stroke one of the bodyguards had felled the High Priest. His dead body dropped in front of the golden throne.

Then began one of the worst slaughters in history.[1] Thousands of Jews sought to flee down the only path available, that of the carpeted passageway leading from the gate to the throne platform. Jews forced their way through the ranks of the President's guards and of the dignitaries on the carpet to flee down this only prospect of an avenue of escape. As they ran the gauntlet through the two ranks of police, one by one they fell. None of the Jews in the Temple courtyard reached the gate. There was no bloodshed, for the police used their *paralyzators*. A slight pressure on the trigger and all motion in the body aimed at was stopped by a paralyzing ray. Every muscle was frozen. Then followed a disintegration of the body as a result of the ray. The flesh was consumed and even the bones crumbled to dust. Within two minutes no vestige of the former human body was visible except a scattering of fine powder where the victim had stood. Soon the purple carpeted path was white with this powder as thousands of Jews met their death and disintegration.

Jews on the walls, in the Temple and close to other exits fled in panic and fear. Then was revealed the perfect organization and preparations that had been made to care for such a contingency. Scattered throughout the vast crowd of people were many thousands of other police in civilian clothes. As they spotted Jews fleeing they shot them down. Even on the Mount of Olives, there too police were posted and the slaughter ran into hundreds of thousands.

Israel had been warned of this event to come. Isaiah Daniel, Jeremiah and the Lord Jesus Himself had told what was coming and what to do at that time. Jesus had said, "I am come in my Father's name, and ye receive me not: if another shall come in his own name, him ye will receive."[2] Jesus had come without deception, claiming to be sent by His Father.[3] He made no claim in Himself to supernatural power and refused personal worship.[4] He gave all glory to His Father, Who dwelt in Him.[5] Yet Jesus warned of one coming who would claim to be God and would demand worship as such.

The evil scheming of this man of sin was now revealed. Not by his own human power but by the power of Satan he had lifted himself in worldly esteem until he had reached the pinnacle of worldly power. Hitler, Mussolini, Stalin — all had risen from obscurity to positions of tremendous power by the spirit of Satan. But this man was different. Here was the incarnation of Satan himself.[6] As Jesus was God manifested in flesh,[7] so this man was Satan — all the evil genius and power of the arch-enemy of God — incarnated in a human fleshly form.[8] This was to be Satan's supreme effort.[9] For this he had schemed thousands of years.[10]

Solomon's Temple had been erected under God's direction upon Mount Moriah. At the time of dedication the Shekinah glory of God had filled the Temple as a cloud. It was here that Jehovah had put His name and received worship as the one true God of Israel. It was to Israel alone that God had revealed Himself.[11] Israel, alone of all the nations, knew and worshiped the true God, Creator of the universe. Here then were manifest the machinations of Satan. On the spot where Jehovah had ordained worship of Himself, Satan had permitted Israel to rebuild their Temple that he might at this place and in a temple erected to God transfer worship to himself. Where Jehovah had put His name Satan set up his image, supernaturally endowed it, and demanded worship as God, showing that he was God.

Thus Satan schemed, but his plans had been known for ages.[12] Prophets had prophesied of this day and Jesus too had warned Israel. "When ye therefore shall see the abomination of desolation, spoken of by Daniel the prophet, stand in the holy place... Then let them which be in Judea flee into the mountains."[13] He had spoken more than nineteen hundred years earlier. His words but echoed the warning of Isaiah. This prophet had advised Israel to gain favor with the ruler of the land extending from Jerusalem to Petra in Edom. "Send the lamb,"[14] he said, a gift. Then to the people of that land he said, "Let mine outcasts dwell with thee... be thou a covert to them."[15] "The daughter of Zion" (Israel) ... shall be "as a wandering bird cast out of the nest,"[16] Isaiah continued. In an involved sentence, continuing to warn Israel, he exhorted them to flee.[17] He promised, however, that the day would come when Israel would finally be restored and the Lord would rule on earth and judge the world in righteousness.[18] Jeremiah had warned of a time to come,

"Alas! for that day is great, so that none is like it: it is even the time of Jacob's trouble." Continuing he promised, "But he shall be saved out of it."[19]

This was the day of which Jeremiah, Isaiah, Daniel, the Lord Jesus and others had prophesied and Satan had fulfilled the prophecies exactly as though they had been used as a pattern. The image and the temple had been erected, Satan had demanded worship as God. Israel had refused to worship him and the slaughter followed. Jacob's trouble had begun.

Chapter Twenty-one

THE FLIGHT!

Jesus had said to the Jews, "pray ye that your flight be not in the winter, neither on the sabbath day."[1] If the Jews prayed, as He advised, their prayers were only half answered. The time of their flight was not in the winter, indeed it was in the best time of the year, when the hills were still green after the winter rains and the severe heat had not yet begun. However, it was on the Sabbath, as had been planned by the one who now threatened the annihilation of the Jewish race. Jesus knew the stress the Pharisee Jews placed upon the Sabbath in His day.[2] He also foreknew the increased stress they would place upon it in the latter days. For rather than lessening the emphasis on Sabbath, orthodox Jews were probably more dogmatic upon their return to Israel than they had been before their exile.

Ever since the setting up of the State of Israel, in 1948, the question of religious observance had been a bone of contention between the orthodox and irreligious Jews. The orthodox desired to impose theocratic rule upon the State. They wanted the Torah to be the sole basis of the law of Israel. They would have ruled Israel in the twentieth

75

century A.D. on the basis of conditions that existed in one thousand B.C.

Fortunately, the actual number of orthodox Jews was small. Though they "flung their weight around" much more than their size would warrant, they never were able to get far in establishing the law of the Torah in the new State.

Their failure to have the Sabbath laws fully observed was not due to lack of trying. From the beginning they had been able to stop bus transportation traffic in Jerusalem. When taxis refused to obey the Sabbath, orthodox Jews, dressed in their Sabbath clothes, long black robes and fur-trimmed hats, lay down on the pavement of the main streets, filling the roadway from curb to curb. Thus they compelled taxis and private cars to cease operating for a while. At one time they made a practice of noting the license numbers of cars driving on Sabbath. Later through the week, they would watch their opportunity and burn the cars.

If a house caught fire on Sabbath the Sabbath-keepers would stop fire engines from going to the fire. Doctors would be stopped, driving to a dying patient, by heavy chains across the road. Ambulances were not permitted to enter orthodox sections to remove sick patients. Electric lights, stoves or heaters could not be turned on in any orthodox home on Sabbath.

Jesus knew these traditionalists would be nineteen hundred years more fanatical when the nation would be re-established in the land. He knew that rather than travel on the Sabbath Day,[3] even to flee from a slaughtering enemy, they would stand in their places and be killed. Knowing this, He had warned them to pray that their flight should not be on the Sabbath. But His words were in vain for the traditionalists.

The great stone image had spoken on the Sabbath and the flight to the Mountains of Edom[4] had begun that day.

Far south in Edom, centuries ago, a people had built themselves a fortress city. Just before the time of the Lord it had been a prosperous trading center. It was at a spot where the main east and west, north and south caravan routes crossed. It was not only a main stopping point to rest and refurnish the caravans, but it was also an important place of trade. Nabatean merchants became wealthy through this exchange.

Petra, (or Sela as the city was called in Bible days),[5] was in the heart of the mountains of Edom. The only entrance to the city was through a narrow defile, one and one-eighth miles long. At places the defile was narrow enough for a man to touch the sides with outstretched arms. The sides went straight up in many places some hundreds of feet. The defile made the defense of the city a simple matter.

At the end of the defile was a beautiful stone building called the "Treasury." From there one entered from the right into the main part of the city. A beautiful view presented itself to the traveler standing in awe before the surrounding mountains. On every hand were great temple buildings and dwelling places. The edifices of Petra were not, strictly speaking, buildings. It would be more correct to call them, "carvings" for each building had been cut out of the face of a mountain. The front of each temple was carved from solid rock, the work of master stone-carvers. The cutting had been executed not only with skill but with great artistry. Inside many of the huge edifices the beautiful coloring of the stone could be seen in parallel streaks of shading and color. Petra had been called, "The Rose-red Rock City."

This was the place that God had prepared for Israel in the wilderness.[6] It probably was an inhabited city in Isaiah's day, when he mentioned it by name and indicated it as the place of refuge. It certainly was existing in the days of Jesus when he warned Israel of a day coming when they should, "flee into the mountains."[7] He told them the sign whereby they should know that the time had come to flee—"the abomination of desolation . . . in the holy place."[8] Their place of refuge had been indicated by Jesus and mentioned by Isaiah—Petra.[9] And Jesus had promised that—"he that shall endure unto the end," (he that shall survive the murderous slaughter, the flight through Moab and Edom, and shall reach the city of Petra) "the same shall be saved."[10]

Of the fanatically orthodox Jews who refused the warning to flee, none escaped. All died. Of the others, most of those in Jerusalem perished. A small remnant, however, from Jerusalem and many Jews who had not gone up to Jerusalem for the unveiling were able to make their way to the city of refuge. Some had private air transportation available, a combination of the flying saucer and helicopter which enabled them to drop right into the fortress city. Others were able to use their many-wheeled land sleds to get close to the city and then abandon their machines to make the rest of their journey on foot. Many of those in the Negev were able to go due east to Petra, some of them in *Rolligons*. Some traveled by night, hiding in caves by day, and eventually reaching the safety of the city of refuge. Amongst those who escaped were some of the leading scientists from Rehovot. Their scientific knowledge was to be put to good use in providing protection for the remnant of Israel in Petra. The chief protection however was to be provided by God Himself.[11] The days were to be shortened and the earthly elect (Israel) would be saved.[12] Here the remnant of Israel would finally reveal their faith in Jesus Christ, the true God of Israel.[13] They would see Him come forth to them. Rending the heavens He would come to destroy the enemies of Israel[14] and to reveal Himself as King of Kings and Lord of Lords, the MESSIAH of Israel.[15]

PART IV

ISRAEL AND THE MESSIAH

> . . . they shall look upon me whom they have
> pierced, and they shall mourn for him, as one
> mourneth for his only son . . .
>
> Zechariah 12:10

Chapter Twenty-two

IN PETRA

Hidden away in the rock caves and tunnelled-out temples and homes of Petra, the Jews waited in fear and trembling. The land of Israel had become prosperous and attractive during the period while the Temple was building, so much so that Jews in America and other countries who had refrained from returning to the land of their fathers prior to the Russian invasion had now all come home. As a result, the whole nation of Israel was back in their land and few Jews were to be found in any other country.[1]

At the time of re-establishing temple worship there had been a tremendous spiritual annointing on large groups of Jews. This happened not only in Jerusalem but in every part of the country. Thousands seemed to be seized with a spiritual fervor causing them to cry unto God, to shout out in ecstasy, or to pass into what seemed to be a trance. With some the trance lasted for several hours. John, while on the Isle of Patmos, had seen in a vision a great sealing of Jews of every tribe.[2] Those who experienced this blessing neither knew what tribe they were of, (except certain ones of the tribe of Levi), nor the significance of what happened to them. It was discovered in Petra, however, that most of those who had reached the safety of that haven had been among those who had the spiritual experience of the sealing.

Following the great religious stir among the Jews in their land, there had been a series of calamities throughout the earth.[3] These occurred in spite of all that could be done to prevent them. Though scientists had learned to control the elements in a measure by radioactive rays, yet there came forth such lightning, thunder and earthquakes[4] that the combined power of all the protective machinery had no effect in checking nature at this time. Later, further storms followed, and vast areas were blanketed with tremendous sized hailstones bringing destruction of property and loss of life to millions.[5] Most fearful of all was a great flaming meteor which plunged into the middle of the Atlantic Ocean.[6] Estimates of the size of the meteor ranged from one hundred to five hundred miles in diameter. That part of it which remained above the waters of the ocean was a flaming ball of fire glowing for several days and finally becoming a bare, rocky island. The tidal waves resulting from the plunging of this mass into the sea created havoc along the shores, both in Europe and America, and in some places passed many miles inland. Yet none of the catastrophes seemed to affect seriously those who escaped.[7] Millions perished, yet life continued, damage was quickly restored and conditions were soon normal.

None of those Jews who had experienced the spiritual phenomena had been affected by the disasters.[8] Indeed life had changed completely for them since their ecstatic experience. Earthly conditions and happenings seemed to mean little to them now. They appeared to be constantly on the alert as if in expectation of something about to happen. What that something was eventually showed itself to be the revelation of the Man of Sin and the subsequent Jewish rejection and flight for safety. All

Jews who had shared in the spiritual experience escaped any harm or injury, as though they had been branded or sealed, a people set apart by God.[9]

When the terrible slaughter began these sealed Jews were prepared and ready and none failed to reach the place of refuge in the mountains of Edom. None, that is, who felt moved to heed the Lord's warning and to flee to the place of safety. But many felt that God had a special work for them to do yet in Israel. With the revelation of the wicked one many Jews unable to reach Petra, or uninformed of the protection that it offered, had continued in their villages and settlements. Many of these had been slain in the days following the unveiling in Jerusalem, but a considerable number, in the aggregate, survived. They were able to continue to live although to do so many had to hide themselves by day.

It was to this remnant of Jews surviving in caves, in villages off the beaten track, or even hiding in towns and cities, to whom some of the sealed Jews felt a special calling. When the time had come for Israel to accept the Antichrist or to suffer the consequence of rejection the specially called among the sealed ones had revealed their faith in Jesus Christ as the Messiah of Israel and the Saviour of the world. They were chosen ones and they carried the burden of revealing Christ to those among Israel who had not heard the Gospel. "...they loved not their lives unto the death."[10] They were sought out by the World Police, beaten, tortured, slain.[11] Yet those surviving continued their ministry as long as they had strength or breath. They were those of whom the Lord had spoken, "But when they persecute you in this city, flee ye into another: for verily I say unto you, Ye shall not have gone over the cities of Israel, till the Son of man be come.[12] They and those who believed with them were martyred, but the Gospel light continued to shine.

Among those of the "sealed" Jews who reached Petra

none up to this time had made a public confession of faith in Jesus. What their actual spiritual condition and faith were had yet to be revealed. They were well informed about the contents of the New Testament. Many had brought small New Testaments with them in their flight. Others were overjoyed to find that someone had unearthed a store of these books in Petra. They were those placed there decades ago by W. E. Blackstone, and later by Dr. Chas. S. Price. These men, among many others, had rightly divided the word of truth and anticipated Petra as the refuge it now proved. The New Testaments had been buried in air-tight sealed containers in preparation for this event. By good fortune (or did God lead them to it?) the treasure was discovered soon after their arrival. Those who were not on guard or occupied with necessary tasks spent their time in an earnest study of the Holy Word.

Chapter Twenty-three

THE FURY OF ANTICHRIST

Through the years there had been a great change in the Arab nations. No longer were their armies weak and ineffective. Great strides had been made in improving the condition of the *fellaheen.* All children in Arab lands were enrolled in school and illiteracy had dropped to a low percentage. One thing had not changed, they never wavered in their hatred of Israel and the Jews.[1] The flight from their homes of hundreds of thousands of Arabs in 1948 as a result of the unprovoked Arab attack on the Jews, had never been forgotten. Though the Arab leaders themselves had been to blame for the flight they put the blame on Israel. By now all the refugees were reestablished, comfortable and prosperous, yet there still rankled a bitter, implacable spirit of enmity against Israel and a supreme desire for revenge. As a matter of fact, for four thousand years Ishmael had never ceased to be jealous of Isaac and to mock him,[2] nor had Esau ceased to hate Jacob and to covet his position with God.[3]

The flight of the Jews to Petra, in the heart of Arab country, was an affront and presented an opportunity for long desired revenge. The Arabs were not slow to react. Encouraged by the World Leader they mobilized all their armies and began a supreme effort against the Jews in Petra and those who remained in Israel.[4]

Immediately following the flight of the Jews, Arab civilians had begun to move into Israel from surrounding countries. It began, at first, among a few of those who had formerly lived there. Then, as word was sent out, a considerable movement began as Arabs rushed to obtain the spoil of beautiful homes, modern equipment and fine farms left by the Jews who were slain or had fled to Petra.

Now the Arab armies were mobilized at full strength. The fury and wrath of Satan was revealed as he urged on the Arab leaders in their hatred of the Jews and determination to annihilate them.[5] Near the site of ancient Bozrah,[6] north of Petra, hundreds of thousands of Arab soldiers were encamped. This was headquarters for the attack. A great airfield had been built and the first attempt against the Jews was to blast them out from the air. A mighty armada of planes assembled and took off. They were loaded with powerful bombs and other death dealing instruments.

Squadron after squadron of planes passed over the main base and headed directly for Petra, but a few miles away. They had orders to fly low and to release all their bombs. Nuclear bombs were not to be used because of the nearness of the target and the danger from radioactive fall-out to the immense troop camps nearby.

On moved the mass of planes until the first flight reached

a point less than five miles from the target. Suddenly, watchers on the ground saw the leading planes shoot skyward at a tremendous speed. Many planes were tossed over on their backs; their wings were wrenched off and the planes crashed to the earth, their bombs causing tremendous explosions and fires. Other planes were carried right out of sight into the sky. Flight after flight followed and experienced the same catastrophic results. Not one plane was able to penetrate what seemed to be an invisible wall. It was as though there was a great updraft from Petra and the borders around it. A stream of air seemed to flow at such a speed that it formed an impenetrable wall. Any plane which approached the edge of this updraft was caught and whirled like a match in a whirlpool.[7] Only a few planes reached their home bases. The destruction had been almost complete and not a bomb had dropped on Petra.

The destruction of their air force caused consternation in the ranks of the Arab leaders. But the anger and fear of the Arabs was nothing compared with the fury and rage of the World Leader. At the zenith of his power and ambition — to be defied by a handful of Jews, to see the Arab air force wiped out without the Jews firing a shot or sending up a single plane in defense — this was a defeat that Satan could not stomach. He determined on the maximum of effort, an all-out attack which must overwhelm the Jews.

Great atomic cannons were brought up and set in position. Hundreds of thousands of troops were massed, ringing Petra around on all sides. Equipped with all the latest small arms, mortars and automatic guns, paced by thousands of tanks and armored cars, the whole force mounted in mechanized transport, they presented a formidable force, one to bring fear to their enemies.

The Jews were more or less unaware of the preparations made against them. They had fortified the Siq, the long narrow defile which led into their fortress, but otherwise there was little they could do. They were vulnerable from above, except that in time the scientists among them were able to construct ray defenses against air attack. But when the Arab air force had been wiped out the Jews knew little of what was going on. The sun had been hidden for some hours as what seemed a great cloud overhung Petra. There had been a violent windstorm which, however, did not harm the Jews who were hidden in their rock shelters. Night and day they were praying to God. He was their only hope and almost their only defense.[8]

Zero hour for the massive Arab attack arrived and everything began to move with military precision. A great wave of military might swept on to engulf and swallow up the handful of Jews. Satan was banking on the success of this great effort. Here was all that stood between Satan and complete earth domination. If the Jews could be eliminated, the promises of God would become impossible of fulfillment.[9] The Word of God would be proved untrue, God would be dishonored and Satan would rise triumphant as the God of heaven and of earth. There seemed no hope for the Jews from a natural standpoint. Their only hope was a spiritual defense. Thus it became a struggle between the forces of righteousness and the forces of evil; between God and Satan.[10]

On moved the mighty army. Soon, as their advance began to gain momentum, the great artillery barrage began. A great curtain of fire rose up from all sides and concentrated on Petra. The guns had only begun to find accurate range when suddenly the earth shook, deep fissures opened and guns, tanks, motor vehicles and tangled masses of humanity disappeared into the bowels of the earth.[11] The few troops which escaped death as the jaws of the great fissures closed again, crushing all within, were so completely paralyzed by fear that they were unable to move. Eighty per cent of the immense force of men were killed and the remainder incapacitated for war. God's victory was complete and once more He proved Himself the defender of His people. As reports of the disaster reached Washington the countenance of the President became livid with rage. The vileness of his words and the terribleness of his threats struck fear into all hearts.

Chapter Twenty-four

ISRAEL'S CRY

Conditions on earth for the people of the world had changed considerably since the unveiling in Jerusalem. No longer was the World Leader the suave, diplomatic personality he had shown himself to be before. No longer was any attempt made to hide the hard, cruel nature within. He ruled now with a rod of iron.[1] People either submitted or suffered death as an alternative. Those who refused to submit were deprived of their homes, their livelihood and the possibility of purchasing the necessities of life.

In order to ferret out those who would not yield to the President's dictates, an order was issued commanding that all people should immediately apply to special offices opened in every center of population. There temporary cards and numbers would be issued. Following this, and as speedily as medical centers could handle them, each individual must report as called by his number. At these medical centers a special mark was to be tattooed on the forehead or on the back of the right hand of everyone.[2] All, from the greatest to the least, were to submit themselves. The only exceptions were to be children under two years of age. When they reached their second birthdays they too must be taken to the medical center for similar branding.

This branding was reminiscent of Hitler's numbering of the Jews in concentration camps during the Nazi regime, years before. There were Jews in Petra still bearing

Hitler's blue tattooed numbers on their arms. It never wore off, even as memories of Hitler's sadism remained indelibly stamped on minds that had suffered.

The brand was a triangle with a peculiar device in the middle. Without this mark none could buy or sell, work or study, live in houses or walk the streets. The mark immediately obligated the wearer to bow down to the images, small sized replicas of the Jerusalem stone image, erected everywhere. Failure to do so brought immediate death, in spite of the mark.

From this time on life not only became unbearable because of regimentation, but terrible plagues continued to fall upon different parts of the earth and few if any were unaffected by them.[3] Terrible sores broke out upon the bodies of people in widely separated parts of the world.[4] Waters in many places turned to a deep red hue and gave off an evil odor, so repulsive that people fell seriously ill from it, or died.[5]

After a year of no rain in certain parts the temperature began to rise so that the heat became unbearable. People were unable to work, except in airconditioned buildings, and even in these it was impossible to keep out the terrible heat. Hundreds of thousands died from heat prostration and sunstroke. There seemed no way of escaping the intensity of the heat. Men cursed God and blasphemed His name, and died.[6]

Though Roman Catholic leaders had rejoiced in their ascendancy and final earthly control through the rise of the World Leader, worship of God had more or less ceased, and all honor and worship had been transferred to the President, yet there still remained a memory of Romanism as a religion of God. There had been much dissatisfaction among both priests and laity at the abolition of traditions and traditional worship. This dissatisfaction had smouldered for years and now suddenly burst into flame. Rome sought to reassert herself and to put herself in the saddle of power.

The purple and scarlet robes of office, decked with

beautiful jewels, had been a symbol of power and control. The Presidential Committee of seven ecclesiastics had rejoiced in the symbol and they had asserted their authority on every occasion.[7] They, and all that they represented, had long been hated and detested by the committee of ten world sub-rulers, who had submitted to the authority of the seven,[8] for they had no other choice.

Now the ecclesiastics decided on a further bid for power. They would demand the revival of worship of the God of heaven through Mary, the Roman deified *Mother of God*. They would put the President in his place as a secular leader, to be subservient to them as the religious leaders. Thereafter they would be the supreme authority on earth.

The plan was well advanced and ready to be put into operation when the Man of Sin discovered what was going on behind his back. Consternation fell upon the members of the committee and other Roman leaders as they realized that nothing could be hidden from the evil one. Yet they tried to gloss it over and to show that they were loyal to the President and had been working on his behalf to strengthen his position.

On the orders of the World Leader, at one fell swoop, the Presidential Guard under the direction of the Committee of Ten,[9] slaughtered the whole ecclesiastical committee and every church leader, however insignificant his position.[10] The word of the Lord was fulfilled, "Thus with violence shall that great city Babylon be thrown down, and shall be found no more at all."[11]

While the world was being racked by plagues and the iron rule of Antichrist, the Jews continued hidden away in Petra. Their plight was pitiful and fearful with no one in all the world to help them or to speak for them. In the brightness of day they longed for darkness to hide them from the eyes of their enemies. By night they longed for day to drive away the dark shadows of fear. They cried unto God:[12]

Look down from heaven, and behold from the habitation of thy holiness and of thy glory: where is thy zeal and thy strength, the sounding of thy bowels and of thy mercies toward me? are they restrained?. . .

O Lord, why hast thou made us to err from thy ways, and hardened our heart from thy fear? Return for thy servants' sake, the tribes of thine inheritance.

The people of thy holiness have possessed it but a little while: our adversaries have trodden down thy sanctuary.

We are thine: thou never barest rule over them; they were not called by thy name.

Oh that thou wouldst rend the heavens, that thou wouldst come down, that the mountains might flow down at thy presence,

As when the melting fire burneth, the fire causeth the waters to boil, to make thy name known to thine adversaries, that the nations may tremble at thy presence!

When thou didst terrible things which we looked not for, thou camest down, the mountains flowed down at thy presence. . .

But we are all as an unclean thing, and all our righteousnesses are as filthy rags; and we all do fade as a leaf; and our iniquities, like the wind, have taken us away.

And there is none that calleth upon thy name, that stirreth up himself to take hold of thee: for thou hast hid thy face from us, and hast consumed us, because of our iniquities.

But now, O Lord, thou art our father; we are the clay, and thou our potter; and we are all the work of thy hand.

Be not wroth very sore, O Lord, neither remember iniquity for ever: behold, see, we beseech thee, we are all thy people.

Thy holy cities are a wilderness, Zion is a wilderness, Jerusalem a desolation.

Our holy and our beautiful house, where our fathers praised thee, is burned up with fire: and all our pleasant things are laid waste.

Wilt thou refrain thyself for these things, O Lord? Wilt thou hold thy peace, and afflict us very sore?

And God shortened the days for them.[13]

Chapter Twenty-five

HEAVEN ANSWERS

As Israel travailed in anguish on earth, marvelous events were taking place in heaven. The Church, spiritual Israel, which long before had been caught up to heaven to meet the Lord,[1] was rejoicing and marveling at the glory and beauty of the Lord as revealed to them by His presence.[2] The judgment of the Church had been completed, and each had received his reward, great or small.[3] Now, the most wonderful event was to take place — the marriage supper.[4]

None of those attending had failed to provide themselves with the marriage robes—fine linen pure and white.[5] As the heavenly music swelled to a glorious crescendo the Lord appeared. The praises of the saints, the hallelujahs of the Church were as the voice and thunderings of many waters.[6] No earthly mind could conceive the beauty and majesty of the Lord. No words nor brush could paint a picture so absolutely glorious.

Nothing of what was transpiring on earth was known to the raptured saints. Their thoughts were entirely on the Lord and on heavenly things. It was all so completely wonderful that everyone was filled with feelings of awe and humility. The marriage supper was a banquet sumptuous beyond any natural understanding.

The Lord, however, was not uninformed of earthly matters. He knew of the revelation that had taken place of the Man of Sin. He knew of the plight of the Jews and their flight to Petra. He had defended them against all the efforts of the Arabs to overcome them.[7] He knew their sufferings and their fears. He heard their cry.

The time had come for one of earth's most important events. Now Heaven was to come down to earth. John's apocalyptic vision was about to be fulfilled; the Lord was returning.[8]

Heaven was opened, the clouds rolled back, and forth came a glorious procession such as earth had never before witnessed — The Lord and His saints.[9]

> His eyes were as a flame of fire, and on his head were many crowns; and he had a name written, that no man knew, but he himself.
>
> And he was clothed with a vesture dipped in blood:[10] and his name is called The Word of God.
>
> And the armies which were in heaven followed him upon white horses, clothed in fine linen, white and clean.
>
> And out of his mouth goeth a sharp sword, that with it he should smite the nations: and he shall rule them with a rod of iron: and he treadeth the winepress of the fierceness and wrath of Almighty God.
>
> And he hath on his vesture and on his thigh a name written, *King of Kings, and Lord of Lords.*[11]

The Arabs, after their defeats, had persisted in their determination to wipe out the Jews. They had trained and gathered fresh troops and equipment and were in the midst of plans for their "third round" against Israel. At the same time Satan himself had determined to personally take part in this "final" attack.[12] There was to be no mistake or defeat this time. Armies of the nations were being gathered from all over the world. The land of Israel was full of troops — red, yellow, black and white.[13] The size of their armies and the might of their power seemed ridiculous against such a small number of people. But this was no ordinary enemy. Regardless of its size, its strength and defender was Jehovah God, and nothing but an all-out effort could overthrow it.

So the armies assembled. Their war equipment, planes, tanks, giant guns, guided missiles, ray-guns; all the latest inventions of man were there for this final showdown. Israel cried unto God in ignorance of the actual plans of her enemies, yet conscious of the tremendous spiritual force pressing upon her.[14]

> For my sword (power of judgment) shall be bathed (saturated,

filled to the full) in heaven: behold, it shall come down upon Idumea (Edom), and upon the people of my curse,[15] to judgment.

The sword of the Lord is filled with blood, it is made fat with fatness, and with the blood of lambs and goats, with the fat of the kidneys of rams: for the Lord hath a sacrifice in Bozrah, and a great slaughter in the land of Idumea (Edom)...For it is the day of the Lord's vengeance, and the year of recompences for the controversy of Zion.[16]

Ezekiel confirmed this decision of God in the thirty-fifth chapter:

Thus saith the Lord God; Behold, O mount Seir, I am against thee, and I will stretch out mine hand against thee, and I will make thee most desolate.

I will lay thy cities waste, and thou shalt be desolate, and thou shalt know that I am the Lord.

Because thou hast had a perpetual hatred, and hast shed the blood of the children of Israel by the force of the sword in the time of their calamity, in the time that their iniquity had an end: . . . Thus will I make mount Seir most desolate, and cut off from it him that passeth out and him that returneth.

And I will fill his mountains with his slain men: in thy hills, and in thy valleys, and in all thy rivers, shall they fall that are slain with the sword...

And thou shalt know that I am the Lord, and that I have heard all thy blasphemies which thou hast spoken against the mountains of Israel, saying, They are laid desolate, they are given us to consume...As thou didst rejoice at the inheritance of the house of Israel, because it was desolate, so will I do unto thee: thou shalt be desolate, O mount Seir, and all Idumea (Edom), even all of it: and they shall know that I am the Lord.[17]

From heaven poured forth the armies of God, the power of God — a sharp sword out of his mouth.[18]

". . . the Lord hath a sacrifice in Bozrah, and a great slaughter in the land of Idumea (Edom)."[19]

Down upon the defenseless heads of the Arab armies, mostly quartered north of Petra, near Bozrah, rained the judgment of God.[20] None escaped. Out into Arab lands the curse spread, engulfing Arab leaders and people alike.[21]

"For it is the day of the Lords' vengeance, and the year of recompences for the controversy of Zion."[22]

Then into the heart of Petra the Lord advanced with His great host of saints. The Jews could be heard praying and crying on every hand,[23] but a blast on a silver trumpet brought them running. From every part of the great enclosure, from temple, house and cave they poured forth. Young and old, men and women, children of all ages, all gathered to greet the mighty host. One glimpse of the Lord Himself, and they fell on their knees. Then began a wailing and mourning which filled the air, echoing back from wall to wall. "And they shall mourn for him, as one mourneth for his only son, and shall be in bitterness for him..."[24]

Soon a great shout arose — "Lo, this is our God; we have waited for him, and he will save us: this is the Lord."[25] Then once more they fell on their faces and wept as they realized the enormity of the sin of their fathers and of theirs, too. To have rejected such a holy, lovely, compassionate Saviour was more than mind could think on. Tears coursed down their cheeks, they beat their breasts, they cast dust on their heads and mourned and cried without stopping. But the Lord had promised, "...to comfort all that mourn;

To appoint unto them that mourn in Zion, to give unto them beauty for ashes, the oil of joy for mourning, the garment of praise for the spirit of heaviness."[26]

His tender sweet smile encouraged them. He spoke words of endearment and love to them. Soon they were on their feet, faces shining, hands raised to heaven and praises on their lips, until the volume of praise equaled and exceeded their former mourning.[27] The shouts of the Jews were joined by those of the accompanying saints and soon the volume of praise became as thunder, as the sound of mighty waters. There was an ecstasy of rejoicing which welled up in one majestic organ chord of heavenly music, beautiful beyond words.

The saints moved among the enraptured Jews. They were preparing them for the triumphant return to Jerusalem.[28] The controversy of Zion was to be completely settled and Israel was to be permanently restored.[29] The Lord had come — "to bind up the brokenhearted, to proclaim liberty to the captives, and the opening of the prison to them that are bound; To proclaim the acceptable year of the Lord, and the day of vengeance of our God."[30]

A grand procession began to form the Lord leading the way,[31] the Jews and saints intermingled following Him. The Song of Solomon revealed the picture. "Who is this that cometh up from the wilderness, leaning upon her beloved?"[32] But Isaiah gives us the clearest picture of all as he gazes from Jerusalem through the prophetic telescope. "Who is this that cometh from Edom, with dyed garments from Bozrah? this that is glorious in his apparel, travelling in the greatness of his strength?"[33] Then the answer of the Lord echoing back, as the vast procession slowly approaches Zion, "I that speak in righteousness, mighty to save!"

Onward swept the mighty throng. The ground seemed to smooth itself before the feet of the Creator.[34] The stones crumbled to powder and fertilized the soil. The grass sprang up on every hand and flowers burst into bloom as the procession passed by. The birds sang and their song seemed to echo Isaiah's question, "Who is this? Who is this?" Who indeed? Who but the King of Kings and Lord of Lords![35]

Chapter Twenty-six

THE VALLEY OF JUDGMENT

Massed before Jerusalem and back through Sharon and the pass as far as Mount Megiddo the armies of Antichrist awaited orders to move on to the great onslaught.[1] No information of the slaughter of the Arab armies had yet reached Jerusalem. A certain nervous anticipation imbued the forces. Satan knew that it was now or never as far as he was concerned.

"And his feet shall stand in that day upon the Mount of Olives."[2] As the procession approached Jerusalem a cloud[3] covered the city and its environs. Suddenly the cloud lifted and revealed the Lord standing on the Mount of Olives, surrounded by the great host of heavenly and earthly followers. Consternation seized upon Satan and the armies gathered at Jerusalem. "Multitudes, multitudes in the valley of decision . . ."[4] But the time for decision passed, "Out of his mouth goeth a sharp sword. . . ."[5] Soldiers died in their tracks. It was not a battle, though so widely known for centuries as the coming Battle of Armageddon. How could man stand before God?[6] ". . . for I will tread them in mine anger, and trample them in my fury; . . . for the day of vengeance is in mine heart, and the year of my redeemed is come."[7] The armies melted away as snow before a scorching sun. Satan was taken, bound and cast into a great opening in the ground which appeared near Jerusalem. This was to be his abode for the next one thousand years.[8]

While the Lord stood on the mount and the armies of the nations suffered their doom a great shaking of the earth was taking place. Jerusalem was once more laid waste. Not only were the buildings thrown down, but the hills were leveled by the shocks. The Mount of Olives was split in twain and a great valley appeared separating the north from the south half of the mountain.[9] One could now scarcely recognize the old Jerusalem and its topography. All was changed, old landmarks had disappeared, but a new Jerusalem was now to arise.[10]

Chapter Twenty-seven

KING OF KINGS AND LORD OF LORDS

And there shall come forth a rod out of the stem of Jesse, and a Branch shall grow out of his roots: . . .

With righteousness shall he judge the poor, and reprove with equity for the meek of the earth: and he shall smite the earth with the rod of his mouth, and with the breath of his lips shall he slay the wicked.

And righteousness shall be the girdle of his loins, and faithfulness the girdle of his reins.

The wolf also shall dwell with the lamb, and the leopard shall lie down with the kid; and the calf and the young lion and the fatling together; and a little child shall lead them.

And the cow and the bear shall feed; their young ones shall lie down together: and the lion shall eat straw like the ox.

And the sucking child shall play on the hole of the asp, and the weaned child shall put his hand on the cockatrice' den.

They shall not hurt nor destroy in all my holy mountain: for the earth shall be full of the knowledge of the Lord, as the waters cover the sea.[1]

And it shall come to pass in the last days, that the mountain of the Lord's house shall be established in the top of the mountains, and shall be exalted above the hills; and all nations shall flow unto it.

And many people shall go and say, Come ye, and let us go up to the mountain of the Lord, to the house of the God of Jacob: and he will teach us of his ways, and we will walk in his paths: for out of Zion shall go forth the law, and the word of the Lord from Jerusalem.

And he shall judge among the nations, and shall rebuke many people: and they shall beat their swords into plowshares, and their spears into pruninghooks: nation shall not lift up sword against nation, neither shall they learn war any more.[2]

The scene is glorious now. The Temple of Ezekiel's vision is built and stands on ancient Moriah.[3] A throne of purest gold, high and lifted up, is the Lord's place in the Temple,[4] where He will reign for one thousand years. The throne is studded with precious stones — diamonds, pearls, emeralds, amethysts, rubies, etc. It is beautiful to look upon, and yet only a fraction as glorious as His heavenly throne, according to the report of the returned saints.

But, "Where Jesus is, t'is heaven there."[5] Jerusalem itself is now fully rebuilt. It is an international city, for here is earth's "Headquarters." "...out of Zion shall go forth the law...."[6] All nations are represented in this world capital by their most illustrious ambassadors. Beautiful stone buildings have been erected in all parts of the city. The streets have been replanned, trees have been planted and scores of attractive gardens now make the city the most beautiful in the world. Embassy Row is a new parkway leading straight to the Temple. It is bordered by magnificent mansions housing the representatives of the various nations.

There is now a universal law for the whole earth. It is based solely upon "Thou shalt love the Lord thy God, and thy neighbor as thyself." This is the beginning and ending of all law.[7] Any act by any individual or nation which does not measure up to or fulfill this law is severely punished. The world has changed and the people of the world have changed. The population is much less than it was, for many were killed by the great disasters which had struck the earth. Great armies had been wiped out and the destructive fires which had annihilated them had engulfed their home lands, too.

There had been a great judgment of all nations. The basis of judgment had been the actions of these nations toward the Lord's brethren, the Jews, and their treatment of the Jews in their midst[8] during the centuries of Israel's exile. Jesus had said, "... woe to that man by whom the offence cometh!"[9] Now was revealed before all, the intensity of Jewish suffering and the hatred that Satan had inspired against them. Men hung their heads in shame as they realized how terrible had been their feelings and actions against the Jews.[10] They were amazed and ashamed that they had permitted God's enemy to deceive them and mislead them.

There was no nation which had a pure record. There were some whose defense of the Jews at times in their past history offset the evil days, and their judgment was of the lightest. Others were penalized and punished to an extent that they would never again rank as powerful or rich nations. Their fields would produce meagerly, their people would not be strong nor healthy. They recognized this to be righteous judgment and their just deserts.[11]

Soon a phenomenon began to manifest itself among the restored and re-established Jews in Israel. They had rebuilt their land and cities, and Israel was blossoming as never before.[12] Life was glorious and attractive for them. Must more than the natural, however, was the spiritual growth of all the returned Jews.[13]

Through the prophet Hosea, God had indicated the position of the Jews in the last days. "After two days (2,000 years) will he revive us: in the third day (millennium) he will raise us up, and we shall live in his sight... and he shall come unto us as the rain, as the latter and former rain unto the earth."[14] Ezekiel, too, gives the promise of God for this day concerning Israel. "Neither will I hide my face any more from them: for I have poured out my spirit upon the house of Israel, saith the Lord God."[15]

Thus, endued with spiritual power Israel embarks on her task. It was a kingdom of priests which God had created in the beginning, an holy nation,[16] but Israel had never fulfilled her calling. God had called Israel to reveal Him to the world.[17] But Israel had kept Jehovah God to herself and had not even been faithful in her worship of Him. As a result blindness had come on Israel,[19] such blindness as the world had never seen before.

They worshiped Jehovah God, but when their God came to them veiled in flesh they did not know Him.[20] They failed to recognize their Creator.[21] "He came unto his own, and his own received him not."[22] More than that, they

98

actively denied and rejected Him and refused to have Him reign over them.[28]

Now all this was changed. The remnant which had survived had realized the error and sin of their fathers.[24] Then the return and revelation of the Lord had settled the matter forever.[25] This was the King of Israel.[20] Following this they had received the Spirit upon them, as the Church had received it upon the Day of Pentecost,[27] and now they were ready to officiate as the Lord's priests on earth.[28]

Their work, however, was not in the Temple. That work was for the raptured Bride of the Lord.[29] Israel's ministry was to those among the nations still unsaved.[30] It was for this that the Lord had suffered the defection and unfaithfulness of Israel.[31] It was for this that He had preserved them through all the centuries of their exile. It was for this that He had gathered them back to their own land. There He had "weeded out" those who in the last days still persisted in their blindness and rejection of His salvation;[32] leaving a repentant and believing remnant that He could now use.[33]

James had said in Jerusalem that God would raise up the tabernacle of David which had fallen down. He was quoting from Amos.[34] Then he went on to explain just why God would restore Israel. He said, "That the residue of men (all the unsaved on earth) might seek after the Lord, and all the Gentiles (nations), upon whom my name is called (so-called Christian nations), saith the Lord, who doeth all these things."[35]

The purpose of the Lord in preserving and restoring Israel was that she might preach the Gospel and that through her the world would be saved.[36] He had endued the people of Israel with special ability for this purpose.[37] He had given them a persuasive power that no other people possessed, and an ability to convince people of the truth of their message. Now, in the end of the world, in the great Millennial period, they are going forth as missionaries to the ends of the earth. To the great harvest fields in China and Japan, to India and the Middle East, to Africa, Asia, Europe, America and the islands of the sea they go.

Not for these millennial missionaries is the slow plodding and faithful witness of the Gentile Christians in days before the Lord took His Church. Satan is bound now[38] and the lands where he himself had bound people most strongly now offered the choicest fields for the planting of the Gospel seed.

Reports soon came to Jerusalem of mighty revival waves sweeping whole continents. Not by tens, hundreds, nor thousands, but by millions people were turning to the Lord. Whole nations were accepting Christ as their Saviour, repenting of their sins and turning to Jesus.[39]

No longer now was there need of armies, police or human law enforcement. With the Gospel universally accepted, men lived for God, to please and serve Him. Love was the ruling force.[40]

It is true that some did not accept the Lord. Others made a profession but in their hearts rebelled against submitting to Him. These the Lord ruled "with a rod of iron."[41]

Thus we see the Lord vindicated and glorified throughout all the earth.[42] On His glorious throne He rules in Jerusalem.[43] "Of the increase of his government and peace there shall be no end, upon the throne of David, and upon his kingdom to order it, and to establish it with judgment and with justice from henceforth even for ever."[44]

We approach the throne in humility and adoration and join the heavenly voices in singing, "The kingdoms of this world are become the kingdoms of our Lord, and of his Christ; and he shall reign for ever and ever."[45]

FOOTNOTE REFERENCES
Part I

CHAPTER ONE
THE DIASPORA AND
THE PROMISE
1. Ezekiel 22:15; 36:19; Amos 9:9.
2. Isaiah 14:1; Jeremiah 31:7-12; Ezekiel 36:24; Amos 9:14; Jonah 2:4.

CHAPTER TWO
FROM THE EAST
1. Isaiah 43:5.
2. II Chronicles 36:20.
3. Ezra 2:1, 2; 7:6, 7; Nehemiah 2:5-11.

CHAPTER THREE
FROM THE WEST
1. Isaiah 43:5, 6.

2. Deuteronomy 8:18.
3. Ezekiel 36:29.

CHAPTER FIVE
FROM THE SOUTH—
MAGIC CARPET
1. Isaiah 43:6.

CHAPTER SIX
ON EAGLES' WINGS
1. Hosea 3:5.
2. Jeremiah 31:8-11; Hosea 6:1.
3. Isaiah 40:31.
4. Hosea 5:15; Zechariah 8:3.
5. Isaiah 43:6.

CHAPTER SEVEN
ISRAEL TODAY
1. Ezekiel 39:28.
2. Psalm 102:16.

Part II

CHAPTER EIGHT
THE DAY IN WHICH WE LIVE
1. Ezekiel 38:8.
2. Ezekiel 38:8.

CHAPTER NINE
THE COMMUNIST LINE-UP
1. Genesis 10:5.

CHAPTER ELEVEN
THE BIBLE ACCOUNT OF THE
RUSSIAN ATTACK
1. Ezekiel 38:16, 18.
2. Ezekiel 38:3, 16; Joel 2:1, 2.
3. Daniel 7:5.
4. Genesis 10:8-10.
5. Ezekiel 38:8, 16.
6. Ezekiel 38:8, 11, 12, 14.
7. Jeremiah 30:7.
8. Isaiah 33:7.

CHAPTER TWELVE
THE ATTACK
1. Isaiah 33:8, 9; Ezekiel 38:4; Joel 2:3-10.
2. Ezekiel 38:15.
3. Ezekiel 38:9, 15.
4. Joel 2:5.
5. Isaiah 54:17; Joel 2:11-20.
6. Isaiah 33:10-12; Ezekiel 38:19-22.
7. Ezekiel 38:21.
8. Deuteronomy 7:9, 10; Ezekiel 39:4, 7; 38:23.
9. Ezekiel 39:6.

CHAPTER THIRTEEN
WHEN WILL IT BE?
1. Jeremiah 30:7; Matthew 24:15-21.
2. Ezekiel 39:9.
3. Ezekiel 38:5.
4. Matthew 24:44.
5. I Thessalonians 4:16, 17.

Part III

CHAPTER FOURTEEN
THE RAPTURE
1. Matthew 25:6-10; I Thessalonians 4:16, 17.
2. I Corinthians 1:26.
3. Luke 17:34-36.

4. Matthew 24:42.
5. Mark 13:28, 29.
6. Matthew 25:5.
7. Ezekiel 36:24.
8. II Peter 3:3, 4.
9. Ezekiel 38:10.

10. Isaiah 33:1; Ezekiel 38:4-7; Joel 2:20.
11. II Thessalonians 2:7.
12. Ezekiel 38:7; 39:2-6.
13. II Thessalonians 2:3, 4.
14. I Thessalonians 5:3.
15. Psalm 73:4-12; II Thessalonians 2:9-12.
16. John 5:43.

CHAPTER FIFTEEN
THE AFTERMATH
1. Ezekiel 39:4,5.
2. Ezekiel 38:19, 20.
3. Ezekiel 39:4.
4. Ezekiel 38:19.
5. Ezekiel 38:22.
6. Ezekiel 38:21.
7. Ezekiel 39:12.
8. Ezekiel 39:9.

CHAPTER SIXTEEN
A NEW WORLD
1. Ezekiel 39:6.
2. Matthew 25:14-30; Romans 14:10; I Peter 4:17.
3. Ezekiel 38:3; Joel 2:20.
4. Isaiah 34:5-8; Ezekiel 35:2-15.
5. Joel 3:2, 14; Revelation 19:17-21.
6. II Thessalonians 2:11.
7. Revelation 17:3, 18.
8. II Thessalonians 2:4.
9. Revelation 13:1; 17:3, 10-12.
10. II Thessalonians 2:4.
11. Amos 8:12.
12. Daniel 7:25.

CHAPTER SEVENTEEN
THE MIDDLE EAST SITUATION
1. Ezekiel 39:11.
2. Ezekiel 39:12.
3. Ezekiel 39:9.
4. II Thessalonians 2:3, 4.
5. Daniel 9:27.

CHAPTER EIGHTEEN
JERUSALEM
1. Isaiah 27:6.
2. Isaiah 35:1.
3. Daniel 9:27.
4. Daniel 9:26; Micah 3:12; Matthew 24:2; Luke 19:43, 44.
5. Hosea 3:4, 5.
6. Isaiah 61:3.
7. II Samuel 24:18,19; I Chronicles 21:18; II Chronicles 3:1.

8. II Chronicles 6:6; 7:1.

CHAPTER NINETEEN
RENDING THE VEIL
1. Isaiah 27:6.
2. Isaiah 34:8.
3. Ezekiel 38:20.
4. Revelation 13:18.
5. I Chronicles 28:11-21; 29:1, 2; II Chronicles 3:1.
6. II Chronicles 7:1-4.
7. II Chronicles 36:18, 19; Psalm 79:1; Matthew 24:2.
8. Deuteronomy 4:27; Ezekiel 36:19; Hosea 3:4.
9. Revelation 13:15.
10. II Thessalonians 2:4.
11. Revelation 13:13.
12. Revelation 13:16, 17.
13. Revelation 13:15.
14. Revelation 13:8, 15.

CHAPTER TWENTY
TO YOUR TENTS!
1. Jeremiah 30:7; Zechariah 13:8; Matthew 24:21.
2. John 5:43.
3. John 6:38, 39.
4. Matthew 19:16, 17.
5. John 10:38; 14:10.
6. Daniel 8:24.
7. John 1:1, 14; Colossians 2:9; I Timothy 3:16.
8. Revelation 13:2, 4.
9. Revelation 12:12.
10. Isaiah 14:12-14.
11. Genesis 17:19; Deuteronomy 6:1-15; Isaiah 63:19; Amos 3:2.
12. Genesis 3:15; Isaiah 14:13; Daniel 11:45.
13. Micah 4:10; Matthew 24:15, 16.
14. Isaiah 16:1
15. Isaiah 16:4.
16. Isaiah 16:1, 2.
17. Isaiah 16:3.
18. Isaiah 16:4, 5.
19. Jeremiah 30:7.

CHAPTER TWENTY-ONE
THE FLIGHT!
1. Matthew 24:20.
2. Matthew 12:1-14.
3. Josephus, *Antiquities of the Jews;* Book XIII, Chapter VIII, footnote page 394.
4. Matthew 24:16.

5. Isaiah 16:1.
6. Revelation 12:14.
7. Matthew 24:16.
8. Matthew 24:15.
9. Isaiah 16:1.
10. Obadiah 14; Matthew 24:13.

11. Isaiah 54:17; Jeremiah 30:8; 31:11.
12. Matthew 24:22.
13. Isaiah 25:9; Zechariah 12:10.
14. Isaiah 34:5-8; 63:4.
15. Revelation 19:11-16.

Part IV

CHAPTER TWENTY-TWO
IN PETRA
1. Ezekiel 39:28.
2. Revelation 7:3-8.
3. Revelation 8.
4. Revelation 8:5.
5. Revelation 8:7.
6. Revelation 8:8.
7. Revelation 9:20, 21.
8. Revelation 9:4.
9. Revelation 7:3.
10. Revelation 12:11.
11. Revelation 12:17.
12. Matthew 10:23.

CHAPTER TWENTY-THREE
THE FURY OF ANTICHRIST
1. Ezekiel 35:5; Amos 1:11.
2. Genesis 21:9; Galatians 4:29.
3. Genesis 27:41; Obadiah 10.
4. Revelation 12:15, 17.
5. Zephaniah 2:8; Obadiah 10.
6. Isaiah 34:6; Amos 1:12.
7. Isaiah 41:16.
8. Psalm 59:9; Isaiah 41:10-14; 63:5, 6.
9. Jeremiah 31:35-37.
10. Isaiah 14:13-15; Jeremiah 30: 23, 24; Ezekiel 28:17; Romans 16:20.
11. Numbers 16:31-33; Revelation 12:16.

CHAPTER TWENTY-FOUR
ISRAEL'S CRY
1. Revelation 12:12; 13:12.
2. Revelation 13:16, 17.
3. Revelation 11:6.
4. Revelation 16:2.
5. Revelation 16:3-6.
6. Revelation 16:8, 9.
7. Revelation 13:1; 17:3-9.
8. Revelation 17:12, 18.
9. Revelation 17:16, 17.
10. Revelation 17:1; 18:8.
11. Revelation 18:21.
12. Psalm 74:1-11; Isaiah 63:15, 17-19; 64:1-3; 6-12; Hosea 5:15; 6:1.

13. Matthew 24:22.

CHAPTER TWENTY-FIVE
HEAVEN ANSWERS
1. John 14:2, 3; I Thessalonians 4:16, 17; I John 3:1-3.
2. Revelation 4:3, 4; 5:9, 10; 14:1-5.
3. Matthew 25:14-30; Romans 14:10; I Peter 4:17.
4. Revelation 19:7.
5. Matthew 22:11; 25:10; Revelation 19:8.
6. Revelation 19:6.
7. Isaiah 25:4; 44:21; Ezekiel 35:10.
8. Acts 1:11.
9. Revelation 19:11-14.
10. Isaiah 63:2.
11. Revelation 19:12-16.
12. Daniel 11:44.
13. Joel 3:9-12; Zechariah 14:2.
14. Isaiah 58:9; 60:15; 64:1.
15. Exodus 17:14; Isaiah 25:10; Ezekiel 35:3.
16. Psalm 137:7; Isaiah 34:5, 6, 8; Obadiah 8-15; Micah 4:11-13.
17. Ezekiel 35:3-5; 7, 8, 12, 15.
18. Revelation 19:15.
19. Isaiah 34:6.
20. Isaiah 34:5.
21. Jeremiah 49:1-33; Ezekiel 35: 7-9; Joel 3:19; Zephaniah 2: 8-11.
22. Isaiah 34:8; 41:10-15; Nahum 1:2.
23. Isaiah 63:15.
24. Zechariah 12:10.
25. Isaiah 25:9; Hosea 5:15; Matthew 23:39.
26. Isaiah 61:2, 3.
27. Isaiah 12:1-6; Hosea 6:1-3.
28. Isaiah 60:1, 2.
29. Amos 9:14, 15.
30. Isaiah 61:1, 2.
31. Isaiah 35:10; 40:9-11.
32. Song of Solomon 8:5.
33. Isaiah 63:1.
34. Isaiah 40:3-5; 45:12; 51:11;

103

62:10, 11; Habakkuk 3:3-5.
35. Psalm 24:7; Revelation 19:16.

THE VALLEY OF JUDGMENT

1. Isaiah 34:1, 2; Joel 3:1, 2, 9-12; Zephaniah 1:14-18; 3:8; Revelation 16:16; 17:14; 19:19.
2. Zechariah 14:4; Nahum 1:15.
3. Acts 1:9, 11.
4. Joel 3:2, 14.
5. Habakkuk 3:6; Revelation 19:15.
6. Isaiah 66:15, 16; Jeremiah 25:31-33; Nahum 1:6; Habakkuk 3:10-16; Malachi 4:1; Revelation 19:21.
7. Isaiah 63:3, 4; Colossians 2:15.
8. Revelation 20:2, 3.
9. Isaiah 24; Habakkuk 3:10, 11; Zechariah 14:4, 5.
10. Isaiah 40:4, 5; Zechariah 14:10.

CHAPTER TWENTY-SEVEN
KING OF KINGS AND LORD OF LORDS

1. Isaiah 11:1, 4-9.
2. Isaiah 2:2-4.
3. Psalm 48:1-3; Isaiah 24:23; Ezekiel 40:1-4.
4. Ezekiel 43:4-7; Zephaniah 3:14, 15; Matthew 19:28; 25:31.
5. Isaiah 25:8.
6. Isaiah 2:2, 3; Obadiah 21; Micah 4:1, 2.
7. Matthew 22:36-40; Galatians 5:14.
8. Matthew 25:31-46.
9. Matthew 18:7.
10. Lamentations 1:12.
11. Isaiah 11:2-4.
12. Isaiah 14:1-3; 41:18-20; Ezekiel 36:35.

13. Obadiah 17; Zephaniah 3:17.
14. Hosea 6:2, 3.
15. Ezekiel 39:29.
16. Exodus 19:6; Deuteronomy 7:6, 7.
17. Isaiah 41:8, 9; 43:7, 10; 49:6.
18. Hosea 10:1.
19. Isaiah 6:9-12.
20. Isaiah 9:6; Matthew 13:54-56; John 5:18.
21. John 1:3, 10; Colossians 1:16.
22. John 1:11.
23. Matthew 26:63-67; John 19:14, 15.
24. Isaiah 52:6; 64:7; Hosea 5:15; 6:1; Zephaniah 3:11.
25. Isaiah 25:9; 53:10; Ezekiel 35:11.
26. Zechariah 9:9.
27. Acts 2:4.
28. Isaiah 61:6.
29. Revelation 5:10.
30. Acts 15:16, 17.
31. Ezekiel 36:20-22.
32. Revelation 7:3.
33. Isaiah 64:8.
34. Amos 9:11; Acts 15:16.
35. Acts 15:17.
36. Genesis 12:3.
37. Exodus 19:5; Psalm 135:4; Isaiah 41:8-10.
38. Revelation 20:2.
39. Psalm 2:8; Jeremiah 31:34; Zephaniah 3:20; Zechariah 8:23.
40. Isaiah 11:6-10; Ephesians 4:13.
41. Isaiah 11:4; Revelation 19:15.
42. Zechariah 14:9.
43. Isaiah 66:23; Zechariah 2:10-12; 8:3.
44. Isaiah 9:7.
45. Obadiah 21; Revelation 11:15.